SECRETS OF ECLAIRS

For Jérôme and Antoine
To my sister, my mother and my father

PREFACE

Choux is a pastry that's unlike all others.

In the first place, it is one of the only pastries that is prepared "over heat" or, in French, "à chaud", which is very likely the origin of its name: "pâte à chaud" ("hot pastry"). Its originality also lies in the fact that it calls on the talents of the pastry cook (in particular, precision) as much as those of the regular cook (whose intuition plays a major role in making the recipes). Thus, while in any pastry recipe you need to make sure you have the correct quantities of ingredients, it is impossible in the case of choux pastry to know in advance exactly how many eggs you will need. Everything depends on how long the ingredients are boiled in the saucepan and then how much the choux mixture is dried out, and these things are impossible to measure, either in time or in weight. It is above all a matter of observation. Observing the consistency of the mixture before using it: neither too dry, nor too wet, it must stick to the spatula for around ten seconds before dropping off. It's something that can be easily adjusted right at the end of the recipe, as long as you don't get carried away. Everything is explained in detail in this book!

Once the choux dough is ready, you can have fun with the piping bag. Tubes of dough will be transformed into éclairs and then secretly filled with sweet crème pâtissière, or sliced open to hold rosettes of light and pretty chantilly cream. Glossy icing completes the visual delight.

Once your mixture has the right consistency, the whole realm of choux pastry is yours: they won't ever flop again. They will be beautiful, puffed up and golden, ready to be customised in every way and devoured without delay!

TABLE OF CONTENTS

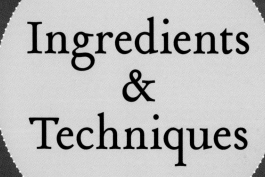

Ingredients
&
Techniques

EGG

THE EGG GIVES THE CHOUX BUN ITS SHAPE, IN EVERY SENSE ...
WHEN IT IS INCORPORATED INTO THE CHOUX MIXTURE, IT BRINGS
WITH IT THE AIR THAT WILL GIVE THE PASTRY ITS ROUNDED
SHAPE. IT ALSO GUARANTEES A BEAUTIFUL GOLDEN CRUST.

COMPOSITION

Generally speaking, the yolk represents 30 per cent of
the weight of the whole egg (or 16 g/½ oz for a large
egg), the white, 60 per cent (or about 32 g/ 1 oz), and
the shell, 10 per cent.

The white, which is 90 per cent water and 10 per cent
protein, is made up of two substances with different
viscosities: a thick white that congregates around
the yolk and a more liquid white located around the
periphery. The fresher the egg, the more thick white
it contains.

The egg yolk is made up of 50 per cent water,
15 per cent protein and 35 per cent fat. It also
contains some carbohydrate and significant amounts
of vitamins A,B , D, E and K. In the recipes in this
book, large eggs are used (53–63 g/2-2¼ oz).

PEAKED EGG WHITES:
EGG WHITES AND SUGAR

To successfully whisk egg whites into peaks, you
need to whisk them on medium speed, add a little
caster (superfine) sugar (poured in gradually in a
light stream) when the peaks start to form and, finally,
whisk on maximum speed. Stop as soon as you can
turn the bowl upside down without the whites
falling out.

WHAT TO WATCH FOR

• Overbeaten egg whites (especially when no sugar
has been added): they become "grainy", which is to
say they take on a curdled appearance. Adding sugar
helps the air bubbles divide: they become smaller and
more numerous. The egg whites are thus firmer and
more stable.

• Adding too much sugar at the beginning: the water
in the egg whites will become viscous and they won't
froth up as easily. The way the sugar is incorporated
is important: too late and you run the risk of grainy
whites; all at once and the whites will collapse.

• The wrong type of sugar: icing (confectioners')
sugar sometimes makes the egg whites too viscous;
standard white (granular) sugar doesn't dissolve well.
Only caster (superfine) sugar should be used.

EGG YOLKS AND SUGAR

When you combine egg yolks with sugar, it is essential
that you whisk the mixture immediately, otherwise the
sugar crystals absorb water and dehydrate the yolk,
which then becomes grainy.

WHEAT FLOUR

YOU CAN'T MAKE CHOUX PASTRY WITHOUT THE INIMITABLE QUALITIES OF GLUTEN, UNIQUELY ABUNDANT IN WHEAT FLOUR.

STARCH

Starch is found in, among other foods, rice, dry legumes, wheat, potato and cassava, which are staple foods in most countries.

Heated in a liquid, starch increases the liquid's viscosity until it reaches a peak. If the individual grains that make up the starch aren't cooked enough, they don't swell up enough to thicken the preparation, which will remain too liquid and leave a floury taste in the mouth. If cooking is continued after peak viscosity is reached, this viscosity diminishes. This is what you are looking for when you make a crème pâtissière: you allow it to boil until it "relaxes". Finally, when you leave the mixture to cool, it thickens considerably. This allows you to make the crème pâtissière, for example, without adding gelatine and extra fat.

GLUTEN

Gluten gives pastry its elasticity, hold, cohesion and gas-retention properties. It ensures the pastry holds together and allows it to rise. This is what we need for choux pastry, which, like bread, needs to rise without baking powder.

WATER

The usual moisture level of flour is about 14 per cent. Excess moisture affects the flour's storage qualities (it may attract mould).

MINERALS

The minerals in flour are located in the outer layer of the wheat grain, the bran. The more bran retained, the higher the mineral content of the flour. Plain (all-purpose) flour, for example, contains fewer minerals than strong or bread flour.

FLOUR AND CHOUX PASTRY

For choux pastry, it is recommended you use plain (all-purpose) flour, sifted.

BUTTER

BUTTER GIVES CHOUX PASTRY ITS FLAVOUR,
COLOUR AND SUPPLE TEXTURE.

CHARACTERISTICS

From a nutritional point of view, fat acts as a high-energy fuel, forms the membranes of our cells and carries the liposoluble (dissolvable in fat) vitamins we need (A, D, E and K). Butter is also an asset on a sensual level: it harnesses flavours, adds softness in the mouth and produces an agreeable sensation of warmth on the palate. Fats can also lead to cardiovascular problems, which is why nutritionists recommend a daily intake of no more than 1 g fat per kilo of body weight.

There are multiple varieties of butter: unsalted, lightly salted or salted. The butter used in the recipes in this book is unsalted butter, unless indicated otherwise, and it may be either pasteurised or unpasteurised as you prefer.

BUTTER AND CHOUX PASTRY

In choux pastry, butter is used for several reasons: it brings flavours and colour that produce a very agreeable taste and look. It lends tenderness to the texture and allows the different components of the mixture to blend together more easily. It also limits the development of the gluten, thus reducing distortion of the shape during cooking (shrinkage). When it is hot, butter melts; as it cools, it solidifies while staying supple, thus contributing to the cohesion of the pastry. Finally, it helps the heat circulate in the pastry, and so optimises the cooking and browning process.

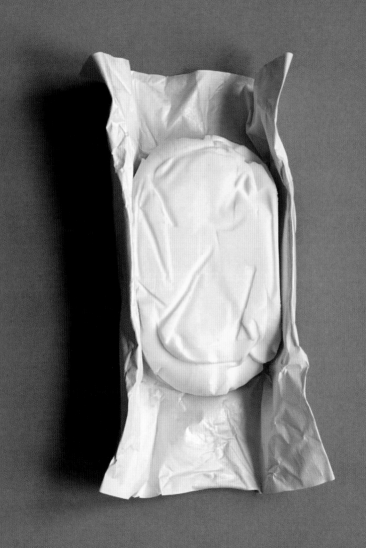

MILK, WATER AND SEASONING

THE KEY TO TEXTURE, THE FINAL TOUCH TO TASTE.

MILK AND/OR WATER

Choux pastry can be made without milk and sugar, but in those cases it is generally intended for savoury recipes. In pâtisserie cooking, the general preference is to replace half of the water with the same quantity of full-cream (whole) milk, and add a little sugar.

SEASONING

Milk gives a richer taste to the pastry and helps to give it a beautiful colour. Salt optimises the flavour. Sugar is also added, but not too much, because it can make the pastry darken too early before the inside has had time to cook through. Take care to dissolve the seasoning (salt and sugar) in the milk/water mixture to ensure it distributes evenly throughout the pastry mixture.

MILK AND WATER + FLOUR

The milk and water is brought to the boil, because only liquid that has reached a temperature of 100°C (212°F) will allow you to achieve a very viscous and lump-free mixture after adding the flour. The flour is incorporated off the heat, so the heat is distributed evenly throughout the mixture, and it is added all at once so that each grain of starch absorbs an equal quantity of water. You need to work quickly once the mixture comes to the boil (large bubbles) to avoid too much water evaporating, because that will change the proportions of the recipe.

REMOVING MOISTURE

When you combine the ingredients together swiftly with a spatula (the loops of a whisk would bend), the grains of starch in the flour absorb water and swell up. This mixture, which is called a "panade", must then be worked over heat to dry out. Reducing the moisture content in this way means you can add the eggs needed to give hold to the pastry without running the risk of a mixture that's too runny.

EQUIPMENT

BEFORE ALL ELSE, GET THE RIGHT TOOLS ...

ELECTRONIC SCALES

Pâtisserie calls for electronic scales, because precision is essential. Since these scales rarely come with measuring units for liquid ingredients, small measures of liquid are given in grams in the recipes.

1 LITRE OF WATER WEIGHS 1 KILOGRAM
15 ML WEIGHS 15 G
This equivalence is not exact for all liquids: oil, in particular, weighs a little less than water, while milk weighs just a little more. In most cases, however, the difference is negligible, so we can consider 1 g = 1 ml regardless of the liquid ingredient.

MIXING BOWL

You need a medium-sized bowl, in particular for whisking the eggs before adding them to the choux pastry. Plastic bowls aren't a good choice for mixing as they absorb flavours and become greasy over time.

FLEXIBLE (SILICONE OR RUBBER) SPATULA

A flexible spatula allows you to thoroughly scrape receptacles holding liquid ingredients. It also allows you to fold mixtures gently to combine them, especially mousses.

WHISK

A whisk allows you to make a lump-free crème pâtissière: whisk constantly just before and during the boiling process.

PLASTIC WRAP

If preparing ahead of time, plastic wrap allows you to create a barrier between the air and your preparation, offering protection from the unwanted side effects of oxidisation: dehydration (and thus the formation of a skin or crust), discolouration and microbial contamination. Some pastry cooks "contact wrap" all of their preparations: they place the plastic wrap directly in contact with the mixture. In this book, this technique is especially recommended for crème pâtissière, which develops a skin as soon as it stops cooking.

BAKING PAPER OR SILICONE BAKING SHEET

It is preferable to use a non-stick baking tray for choux pastries, which means you can avoid using baking paper. In effect, when choux pastries are cooked at 150°C (300°F/Gas 2), they take time to dry out, and the paper will absorb some of their moisture and crumple up. At the end of the cooking time, the base of the choux will be crumpled as well, rather than smooth. If you are nevertheless using a traditional baking tray, a sheet of baking paper (or a silicone baking sheet) will be necessary to stop the pastry from sticking. In this case, it may be necessary in a fan-forced oven to attach the baking paper to the tray so that it doesn't curl up over the choux, either by using small magnets placed in each corner of the sheet, or by dabbing a little choux pastry between the paper and the tray.

OVEN

The ideal is to use a fan-forced oven: there is better heat distribution, it penetrates the choux better, you achieve a better colour and it is not generally necessary to rotate the tray so the choux pastries colour evenly. Make sure air is allowed to escape from the oven (see page 29).

EQUIPMENT (CONTINUED)

FOOD PROCESSOR

The recipes in this book can be made entirely by hand, but they will be easier with a food processor, especially if the quantities are multiplied. The food processor allows the choux pastry dough, which is quite viscous and difficult to work manually, to be mixed vigorously. Choose a processor with a paddle (a paddle is a flat beater) or a blade; a chopping attachment will also work very well. Electric beaters and hand blenders are to be avoided (a whisk isn't suitable for mixing this dough and the blade of a hand blender is too small).

SMALL SAUCEPAN

Unless you are multiplying the basic recipe, a small saucepan (14–16 cm/5½–6¼ inches diameter) is large enough to bring the liquid ingredients to the boil, and then for drying the choux mixture.

STIFF SPATULA

For drying the choux mixture, then for testing its consistency once you have prepared the dough, you need a stiff spatula, in wood or plastic.

BAKING TRAY

If the oven is fan-forced, you can cook several trays at the same time (as long as they are well spaced). The tray should be light because the cooking will be done at a cool to moderate temperature (150°C/300°F/Gas 2); if the tray is too thick, the heat won't distribute evenly under the pastries and their base will become mis-shaped. The ideal is to have a non-stick baking tray; failing that, cover the tray with baking paper or a silicone baking sheet.

OVEN THERMOMETER (OPTIONAL)

Be careful, many ovens are not well calibrated: the displayed temperature may be quite far from the reality. An oven may also indicate that it is preheated when it hasn't yet reached the desired temperature. Since it is important to be precise when cooking pastry, equip yourself with an oven thermometer if possible (available from specialist kitchenware stores or online).

PIPING BAG

You can get re-usable nylon piping bags and plastic disposable piping bags. The latter are very practical, but less ecologically sound than re-usable bags.

PIPING NOZZLE

If you only have one nozzle, it should be a plain 16 mm nozzle, which you can use to pipe just about all the different kinds of choux pastries. For more precision, the recipes in this book call for four plain nozzles (8, 12, 16 and 20 mm diameter), and two star nozzles (6 and 16 mm diameter). The 6 mm star nozzle is optional: it is used to pierce the choux, but the point of any pen works just as well. Nozzles are available in plastic, polycarbonate and stainless steel.

PIPING BAG

ALL YOU NEED TO KNOW ABOUT
THE PIPING BAG FOR PERFECT FILLING ...

EQUIPMENT
1 piping bag
1 nozzle
1 pair of scissors
1 narrow container with high,
   straight sides
1 spatula or pastry scraper
mixture for piping

PREPARING THE BAG
If you are using a disposable piping bag, you have to
cut it first. To do this, open the bag, slip the nozzle
inside and push it down as far as possible, then move
it back up 1 cm (½ inch) and cut the bag at that
point. For both re-usable and disposable bags, place
the nozzle in the hole and push it firmly into place.

FILLING THE BAG
1. Place the bag fitted with its nozzle into the
high-sided container and fold the end of the bag over
the outer edge of the container; that way, the bag is
opened wide. Transfer the mixture into the bag using
a spatula or pastry scraper and wipe the implement
against the edge of the container with each addition
of mixture.
2. Take the piping bag out of the container and
lay it flat on the work bench. Move your hand or,
preferably, a pastry scraper or other straight object
(such as a ruler), along the bag so that you push
the mixture towards the nozzle and leave the rest
of the bag "clean".

3. Take the bag in both hands, point the nozzle
upwards and twist the bag on itself, pushing the
mixture towards the nozzle, so that the mixture
is enclosed as tightly as possible.

IF USING IMMEDIATELY
Continue to twist the bag until the mixture appears at
the tip of the nozzle. Only then do you point the bag
towards the work bench to pipe the mixture.

IF USING LATER
Cover the nozzle firmly with plastic wrap, place the
bag in a sealed container with the nozzle pointing
upwards and, depending on the type of mixture,
place it in the refrigerator or not.

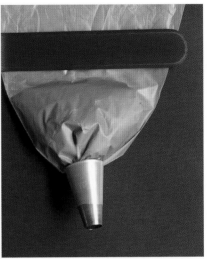

2. Move the mixture towards the nozzle end.

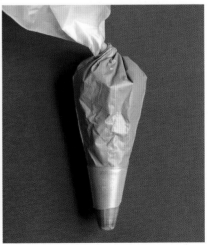

1. Fill the bag cleanly.

3. Twist the bag as close to the mixture as possible.

CHOUX PASTRY IN 4 STEPS

1 / DRYING THE MIXTURE

TO MAKE 6 TO 8 ÉCLAIRS
80 ml (2½ fl oz/⅓ cup) milk
80 ml (2½ fl oz/⅓ cup) water
70 g (2½ oz) butter, diced
large pinch of salt
10 g (¼ oz) sugar
100 g (3½ oz/⅔ cup) plain
  (all-purpose) flour
2 eggs

TO BEGIN

Pour the milk and water into a saucepan. Add the butter, salt and sugar. Place over high heat and stir with a spatula until the butter has melted. Bring to the boil (the butter must be melted before the liquid reaches boiling point) and let it boil for 2 or 3 seconds: the whole surface of the liquid should be boiling with large bubbles. Remove from the heat and add the flour all at once. Start mixing gently (to avoid spatter) then, as the mixture comes together, mix vigorously until you can no longer see any dry flour.

WHY DRY THE CHOUX MIXTURE?

We dry the choux mixture, which is to say we remove excess moisture from it, so it can absorb more egg without becoming too liquid.

HOW TO DRY THE MIXTURE AND MAKE A PANADE

Once you have added the flour all at once (off the heat), and have combined the mixture with a spatula until no more dry flour is visible, you move on to the drying process.
This involves placing the saucepan over high heat and stirring constantly until the mixture no longer sticks at all, either to the saucepan, your fingers or the spatula. Don't hesitate to take the saucepan off the heat once or twice to make sure the base isn't burning. The choux mixture is now ready for the next step! At this stage, it is called a "panade".

A CRUCIAL STAGE

The last stage of the recipe (before shaping the pastry mixture) is adding the eggs. This stage is crucial, because it is the one that will determine whether the pastry is a success or not.

When the mixture is ready to be piped, it must first adhere well to the spatula, then, second, drop off it cleanly. The quantity of eggs you need to add to obtain this consistency depends on how strong the boil was right at the start of the recipe (a few extra degrees and more egg needs to be added to compensate for the loss of moisture) and how much the mixture was dried out afterwards (the more the mixture is dried out, the more egg will be required). There is therefore no hard-and-fast rule and you need to adjust the amount in each individual case.

THE RIGHT CONSISTENCY, CASE BY CASE

Adding egg is essential for the pastry to rise, but too much egg will make the mixture too liquid and prevent it from rising. This is why the second half of the quantity of egg needs to be added little by little. Beat the eggs with a fork and gradually incorporate half of them into the mixture. Test the consistency of the mixture at this point: take some of the mixture on a spatula and lift it up.

• **The mixture passes the test**

If the mixture adheres well to the spatula then drops off with a clean break from the mixture still attached to the spatula (photo 1), it is ready.

• **The mixture is on its way to passing**

If the mixture doesn't stick to the spatula and falls off without leaving any traces behind, or if it doesn't fall off at all, gradually add, in two or three stages, the remaining egg. Re-do the spatula test after each addition until the mixture has the right consistency. Stop adding egg at that point.

• **The mixture fails the test**

If the mixture drops off the spatula straight away (photo 2), too much egg has been added. Most of the time there is nothing more to be done at this point, except to start again!

BEFORE STARTING AGAIN

One chance of success is left: you can try another kind of test. Make a small mound of mixture using a teaspoon or a piping bag and see if the shape holds: if it holds, it's perfect, it doesn't contain too many eggs (photo 3); if it spreads a little (photo 4), you have to start again because the choux won't rise.

THE SPATULA TEST

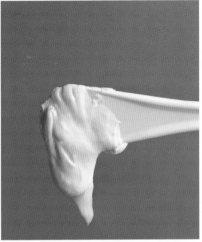

1. The batter passes the test: it drops from the spatula with a clean break.

2. The batter fails the test: it drops off the spatula too quickly.

THE PIPED CHOUX TEST

3. The batter passes the test: the small mound of mixture holds its shape.

4. The batter fails the test: the mound of mixture spreads.

CHOUX PASTRY IN 4 STEPS (CONTINUED)
3 / PIPING THE PASTRY

ÉCLAIRS

Fill a piping (icing) bag fitted with a plain 20 mm nozzle. Position the bag at a 45 degree angle in relation to the tray. A mixture that's a little drier (less egg) will give a result with a more regular shape. When you are making the first éclair, it is a good idea to have a ruler nearby so you know when the éclair has reached the desired length. Push the mixture out of the bag evenly and in a swift motion, keeping in mind that the tube of mixture that comes out should be the same size as the nozzle: if you press too hard it will be fatter; if you don't press hard enough, it will be thinner. Once the éclair is 14 cm (5 ½ inches) long, cut off the mixture, using a smooth-bladed knife for a nice clean result.

BRUSHING WITH EGG

More than the fact that it gives a lovely golden colour to the bun (which is only an advantage when the bun isn't iced), the advantage of brushing with egg is above all that it smooths the surface of the choux pastry. You effectively need to "erase" the irregularities and eliminate the small peak of mixture formed when piping in order to have perfect and smooth icing later. For choux pastries decorated with almonds or sugar, brushing with egg isn't essential, provided you form the choux quickly and apply the decorations straight away. Otherwise, the surface will dry out slightly and won't be sticky any more, and in that case they will need to be glazed.

To glaze, lightly whisk an egg, dip a fingertip (or pastry brush) into the egg and smooth the surface of the choux pastry to make it even. This process can also be carried out using water, as the main aim is to smooth and moisten the dough.

4 / COOKING THE PASTRY

PUFFED CHOUX PASTRY ...

Cooking food in the oven transforms a mixture by subjecting it to heat. The aim is to alter its taste, its texture and even its nutritional qualities, to make it edible or more enjoyable to eat.

When choux pastry is cooked in the oven, the water contained in the pastry evaporates. At the same time, the air that is trapped when the eggs are incorporated expands. These two phenomena result in the pastry puffing up.

Next, the proteins in the egg coagulate, forming a crust on the surface that ensures it all holds together: the choux takes shape and has a stable infrastructure. The proteins in the egg thus play the role of cement in the pastry. If the oven is opened during cooking or if the temperature is too low, the infrastructure doesn't form correctly and the choux collapses.

THAT'S EVENLY COLOURED ...

Using a fan-forced oven is recommended: the heat is well distributed, it penetrates the choux pastry better and you get a better colouring.

Piping the choux in staggered rows and spacing them at least 3 cm (1¼ inches) apart also helps the hot air circulate between them.

VENTILATION

You also need to ensure that air escapes from the oven. To check this, wave your hand in front of the oven while it is turned on to feel whether there is a draught that escapes. If not, you will need to have the oven door slightly open at the end of the cooking time (by propping it open with a wooden spoon, for example) in order to allow the excess moisture to escape and the choux pastry to dry out; this will stop it collapsing once it comes out of the oven. You can also open the oven door a few centimetres and close it quickly at regular intervals, but not until the choux pastries are already well puffed up and coloured.

PIPING THE FILLING

DISCREET vs SHOWY

THE CHOICE OF NOZZLE

This is decided by the recipe: either the filling is hidden inside the pastry, and subterfuge is used to fill it invisibly, or the filling is visible and by contrast the aim is to highlight its indulgent lusciousness. For a hidden filling, choose a plain nozzle, usually medium-sized (8 mm diameter). A nozzle that is too small makes the task of filling quite time consuming, and a nozzle that's too big will make too big a hole in the bottom of the pastry. For a visible filling, choose a star nozzle, smaller or larger in size depending on the effect you want to give the filling.

PIPING A HIDDEN FILLING

Make three holes in the underside of the éclairs by piercing the bottom of the éclair with the tip of a ballpoint pen or a small star nozzle (about 6 mm) that you 'screw' in : one on the left hand side, one on the right and one in the middle. Fill from one of the ends and use the middle hole as an indicator: when the cream is visible through the middle hole, start filling from the other end. Stop when the éclair is nice and heavy and the cream comes out of the holes. Wipe off the excess on the edge of a container and lay the éclair upside down.

PIPING A VISIBLE FILLING

Slice off the top of the choux pastry using a serrated knife and generously fill the other half in a visually appealing way using the chosen nozzle. Place the lid on top of the filling and press very lightly.

GOOD TO KNOW

Choux pastries are always filled before being iced. Once they are filled and iced, refrigerate until serving time.

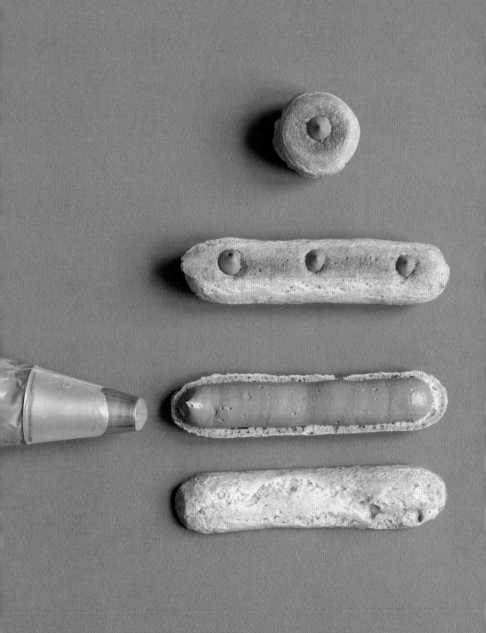

CRÈME PÂTISSIÈRE

A RICH PASTRY CREAM, WITH A LIGHT AND SUBTLE FLAVOUR

CRÈME PÂTISSIÈRE
250 g (9 oz/1 cup) full-cream milk
25 g (1 oz) sugar

EGG-YOLK MIXTURE
3 egg yolks
25 g (1 oz) sugar
pinch of salt
10 g (¼ oz) plain (all-purpose) flour
10 g (¼ oz) cornflour (cornstarch)

THE MILK
Pour the milk into a saucepan. Add the sugar, but wait until you have made the egg-yolk mixture (see below) before placing the saucepan on the heat. The milk shouldn't heat too early, or the amount of liquid will be reduced and the crème pâtissière will be too firm.

THE EGG-YOLK MIXTURE
Place the egg yolks in a bowl with the sugar and salt. Whisk vigorously. Add the flour and cornflour, and combine.

THE MILK OVER THE EGGS
Place the milk over high heat and, just before it reaches boiling point, remove from the heat. Pour a ladleful over the egg-yolk mixture and whisk vigorously; this will allow the sugar to dissolve and loosen the mixture, which will then combine more easily with the rest of the milk.

THE CRÈME ON THE HEAT
Pour the mixture into the saucepan and whisk until smooth. Put the saucepan back on the heat and bring to the boil while continuing to whisk. Once the mixture thickens and has reached boiling point, allow it to boil until the mixture is thick but fluid at the same time (this will take 1—2 minutes maximum). The crème pâtissière is said to have "relaxed" once it reaches this fluid consistency after thickening. Stop the cooking process at this stage.

COOLING AND STORAGE
Transfer the crème to a large plate (to speed up the cooling process) and cover with plastic wrap placed in direct contact with the crème to prevent it forming a skin. This direct contact is necessary to avoid drops of condensation falling back into the crème, and it allows the crème to cool more quickly. Refrigerate the crème as soon as it reaches lukewarm. Once cooled, the crème sets into a mass: it needs to be restored to consistency before use by being whisked vigorously so it becomes soft and creamy again.

The crème pâtissière has reached the right consistency: thick but fluid.

For cooling, place the plastic wrap in direct contact with the crème pâtissière to avoid a skin developing.

FLAVOURED CRÈME PÂTISSIÈRE

VANILLA / CHOCOLATE / COFFEE / CARAMEL

ingredients for 350 g (12 oz)
plain crème pâtissière
(see page 32)
PLUS
½ vanilla bean
½ teaspoon rum, Grand
Marnier or calvados
(optional)

VANILLA CRÈME PÂTISSIÈRE

Split the vanilla bean and scrape out the seeds. Add the seeds, with the bean, to the milk with half the sugar in a small saucepan. Bring the mixture to the boil and, as soon as it reaches boiling point, remove from the heat, cover and allow to infuse for 5—10 minutes. Finish the recipe by following the method for plain crème pâtissière (see page 32). Once it has cooled, incorporate the alcohol if desired. Whisk vigorously until the crème regains a soft and creamy consistency.

ingredients for 350 g (12 oz)
plain crème pâtissière
(see page 32)
PLUS
100 g (3½ oz) dark chocolate
(50—60% cocoa)
85 g (3 oz) pouring (whipping)
cream

CHOCOLATE CRÈME PÂTISSIÈRE

Scald the cream (heat until just below boiling point) in a small saucepan and pour it over the chocolate which has been broken into pieces. Gently stir until you have a thick ganache and set aside. Make a plain crème pâtissière (see page 32) and combine it, still warm, with the ganache. The extra cream in the mixture will compensate for the loss of smoothness due to the chocolate, which hardens as it cools.

Note: if the pouring cream is too hot, the ganache is in danger of splitting (the fat separating out), which is why it is recommended to just scald the cream and not to boil it.

ingredients for 350 g (12 oz)
plain crème pâtissière
(see page 32)
PLUS
2 teaspoons coffee essence

COFFEE CRÈME PÂTISSIÈRE

Make a plain crème pâtissière (see page 32) and incorporate the coffee essence just before cooling, mixing vigorously.

ingredients for 350 g (12 oz)
plain crème pâtissière
(see page 32)
PLUS
85 g (3 oz) pouring (whipping)
cream
90 g (3¼ oz) caster (superfine)
sugar
30 g (1 oz) water
15 g (½ oz) salted butter

CARAMEL CRÈME PÂTISSIÈRE

Make a plain crème pâtissière (see page 32), cover it with plastic wrap and set aside. Scald the cream (heat until just below boiling point)in a small saucepan and set aside. Combine the sugar and water to make a caramel (see page 50) that is quite dark (170–180°C/325–350°F). Remove from the heat, pour in the hot cream and stir in immediately. If the caramel isn't smooth, return to a medium heat for 2 minutes, then remove from the heat and incorporate the salted butter. Transfer to another container and allow to cool to lukewarm. Incorporate the lukewarm caramel into the lukewarm crème pâtissière.

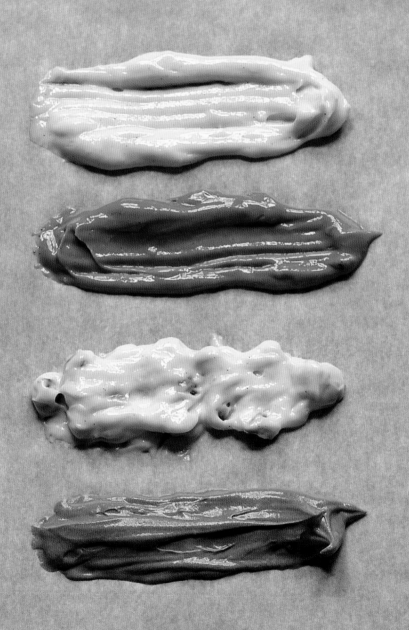

CRÈME MOUSSELINE

A CRÈME PÂTISSIÈRE THAT'S RICH, LIGHT AND GENEROUS

ingredients for 350 g (12 oz)
plain crème pâtissière
(see page 32)
PLUS
120 g (4¼ oz) softened butter

PLAIN CRÈME MOUSSELINE

Make a plain crème pâtissière (see page 32) and, once it is cold, whisk until it has the consistency of a mayonnaise. Whisk the butter until it has the same consistency as the crème pâtissière (mayonnaise). For the two preparations to combine well, they need to be the same consistency but not the same temperature: the crème pâtissière needs to be cold, and the butter lukewarm. Add the soft butter to the crème, then whisk until you obtain a light crème.

ingredients for 350 g (12 oz)
plain crème pâtissière
(see page 32)
PLUS
120 g (4¼ oz) softened butter
60 g (2¼ oz) whole hazelnuts

HAZELNUT CRÈME MOUSSELINE

Make a plain crème pâtissière (see page 32), then a plain crème mousseline (see above). Refrigerate.
Preheat the oven to 160°C (315°F/Gas 2–3). Spread the hazelnuts on a baking tray and toast in the oven for about 30 minutes: they should be very brown, almost black. Remove them from the oven, take them off the tray and allow them to cool.
Grind the hazelnuts in a food processor fitted with a blade; it will take between 3 and 5 minutes, depending on the power of the processor and sharpness of the blade. The paste is ready when it has a liquid consistency. Pour it over the crème mousseline and whisk until just combined.

ingredients for 350 g (12 oz)
plain crème pâtissière
(see page 32)
PLUS
100 g (3½ oz) dark chocolate
(50–70% cocoa)
80 g (2½ oz/⅓ cup) pouring
(whipping) cream
120 g (4¼ oz) softened butter

CHOCOLATE CRÈME MOUSSELINE

Break the chocolate into pieces into a heat-resistant bowl. Scald the cream (heat until just below boiling point) in a small saucepan. Remove from the heat and pour it over the chocolate, then place the bowl over the empty saucepan to help the chocolate melt. Combine using a flexible spatula until the ganache is perfectly smooth. Transfer to another bowl and set aside at room temperature.
Make a plain crème pâtissière (see page 32) and combine, while it is still warm, with the ganache. Cover with plastic wrap placed in direct contact with the crème and keep in the refrigerator until ready to use.
Whisk the cold chocolate crème pâtissière until the mixture has the same consistency as mayonnaise. Whisk the butter until it has the same consistency, add to the crème, then whisk until you have a light cream. Cover with plastic wrap placed in direct contact with the crème mousseline and keep in the refrigerator until ready to use.

Plain crème mousseline and coarsely
chopped hazelnuts.

Crème mousseline with
processed hazelnuts.

CHOCOLATE MOUSSE

AIRY AS A CHANTILLY, SUAVE AS ONLY CHOCOLATE CAN BE

100 g (3½ oz) butter
250 g (9 oz) dark chocolate
(50–70% cocoa)
6 egg whites
40 g (1½ oz) caster (superfine)
sugar
large pinch of salt
4 egg yolks

Dice the butter and place it in a saucepan with the chocolate broken into pieces on top. Place over low heat, then let the chocolate sink into the melted butter and wait for it to melt too. Stir and remove from the heat. Whisk the egg whites to soft peaks. Add the sugar and salt, and whisk some more. The whites should be quite firm.

Place the egg yolks in a mixing bowl and incorporate the chocolate mixture in three stages. Add a quarter of the whisked egg whites, incorporating them gently with a flexible spatula (pass it under the mixture and fold over the top, turning the bowl in the opposite direction). Pour the whole mixture into a shallow bowl, cover with plastic wrap and allow it to set for at least 2 hours in the refrigerator.

CHANTILLY CREAM

LIKE A CLOUD OF FAIRY FLOSS

400 ml (14 fl oz) very cold pouring (whipping) cream (refrigerated for at least 12 hours)
50 g (1¼ oz) icing (confectioners') sugar

CHOOSING THE CREAM

You need a full-fat pouring cream (30 per cent dairy fat), because it is the fat that stabilises the foam. In effect, when you whip the cold cream, the air bubbles you introduce are held by the dairy fat which solidifies around them, this fat being solid when cold.

HOW TO MAKE THE CHANTILLY

COLD – The cream needs to be quite cold before being whipped (4°C/39°F). It is also recommended that you refrigerate the beaters/whisk and the container the cream will be whipped in, and work in a room that's as cool as possible. It is ultimately the cold dairy fat that will solidify and give structure to the chantilly. If it is not cold enough, it won't be able to solidify and the cream won't whip properly.

THE RIGHT CONTAINER – Preferably whip the cream with an electric beater or electric mixer with a whisk attachment. For a small quantity, pour the cream into a small receptacle with high sides that's just large enough to contain the beater. For a large quantity of cream, use a stand mixer if possible; otherwise, pour the cream into a mixing bowl.

WHIPPING – Start whisking on medium speed, then finish on high speed to multiply and divide the air bubbles. When the cream is almost ready, add the sugar and continue to whisk until the chantilly holds up in a generous mass on the loops of the beaters/whisk. Don't whisk any further, at the risk of seeing your chantilly turn into butter!

CHANTILLY CREAM USING A CREAM SIPHON

HOW IT WORKS – A siphon is an aluminium bottle containing, under pressure, a liquid that has been carbonated by carbon dioxide. By operating the lever that controls the flow of liquid, this liquid comes out as a foam. This allows sweetened cream to be instantly transformed into a chantilly.

PROCESS – Pour the cream mixed with the sugar into the bottle. Attach one gas cartridge for a 500 ml (17 fl oz/2 cup) siphon (or two, one after the other, for a 1 litre/35 fl oz/4 cup siphon) and shake the apparatus vigorously so that the gas combines with the liquid and aerates it. Then place the siphon in the refrigerator. At serving time, shake the siphon again and operate the lever to make the chantilly come out of the nozzle. The chantilly will keep this way for several days in the refrigerator.

FLAVOURED CHANTILLY
FLAVOURS AND COLOURS

ingredients for 450 g (1 lb)
chantilly cream (see page 40)
PLUS
1 teaspoon natural vanilla
extract and/or 1 pinch ground
vanilla or 1 vanilla bean

VANILLA
To give a vanilla flavour to chantilly, use vanilla extract or ground vanilla. Vanilla beans are precious and aren't shown to their best advantage in a cold dish: it won't give full expression to their aromatic properties. Whichever vanilla you choose should be added at the same time as the icing sugar.

ingredients for 450 g (1 lb)
chantilly cream (see page 40)
PLUS
1 teaspoon natural vanilla
extract and/or 1 pinch ground
vanilla or 1 vanilla bean
½ teaspoon rum, Grand
Marnier or calvados

ALCOHOL + VANILLA
You can also add one or more types of alcohol, in very small quantities (a maximum of 1 teaspoon each): Grand Marnier, rum or calvados will give depth and complexity to the cream and pair perfectly with the vanilla. Alcohol and vanilla should be added at the same time as the icing sugar (since the alcohol is at room temperature, it will raise the temperature of the cream if added too soon).

ingredients for 450 g (1 lb)
chantilly cream (see page 40)
PLUS
¼ teaspoon violet essence or
1 tablespoon violet syrup
a few drops each of red and
blue food colouring

VIOLET
Liquid food colourings are easier to measure out than food colourings in paste or powder form. They should be added at the very beginning of the recipe for a better "read" of the colour. On the other hand, essence or syrup should be added at the same time as the icing sugar.

ingredients for 450 g (1 lb)
chantilly cream (see page 40)
PLUS
½ teaspoon rosewater
a few drops of red food
colouring

ROSE
Follow the same process as for violet.

CHOCOLATE GANACHE

CREAMY, DENSE, WITH AN INTENSE CHOCOLATE FLAVOUR, FOR FILLING SMALL PIECES OR FOR ICING

DARK CHOCOLATE
125 g (4½ oz) dark chocolate
(50–60% cocoa)
50 g (1¾ oz) butter
40 g (1½ oz) honey
125 g (4½ oz/½ cup) pouring
(whipping) cream

MILK CHOCOLATE
185 g (6½ oz) milk chocolate
35 g (1¼ oz) butter
30 g (1 oz) honey
90 g (3¼ oz) pouring
(whipping) cream

WHITE CHOCOLATE
205 g (7¼ oz) white chocolate
35 g (1¼ oz) butter
25 g (1 oz) honey
75 g (2½ oz) pouring
(whipping) cream

Place the chocolate, broken up into pieces, the butter, diced, and the honey into a heat-resistant bowl.

Scald the cream (heat until just below boiling point) in a small saucepan. Remove from the heat and pour into the bowl over the chocolate.

Gently mix with a flexible spatula until the chocolate and butter have melted. If they don't melt completely, pour 1 cm (½ inch) water into the saucepan you used to heat the cream, bring to the boil, turn off the heat and place the bowl on top.

Mix until the ganache is perfectly smooth.

ICING

THE PERFECT FINISH

THE CORRECT CONSISTENCY

The most important thing when it comes to icing is the consistency.

You can ice choux pastry with lots of different things: fondant, ganache, clear caramel, creamy caramel .... In any of these cases, the icing will only work if the consistency is right, which is to say neither too runny (the icing will take on the exact shape of the choux, revealing its little irregularities, and it will run off without covering the choux properly) nor too thick (the result won't be smooth and you'll be biting into big chunks of sugary substance). The icing also needs to be fluid enough so you can dip the choux into it: don't ice with a spatula if you want the perfect finish. You then have to be able to run a finger around the line of icing for a good clean edge.

FOR FONDANT

Ready-made fondant icing needs to be a little below body temperature (about 35°C/95°F). You also need to add just a tiny bit of lukewarm water to it (between a few drops and a few teaspoons, depending on the amount of fondant used), until the mixture falls back without immediately merging with the rest of the fondant in the saucepan (photo 1).

FOR GANACHE

Use ganache immediately, so it will be at its shiniest.

FOR CLEAR CARAMEL

It will have the right consistency once it stops bubbling.

THE CORRECT ACTION

THE BASIC TECHNIQUE

Dip the choux into the icing (photo 3), hold it upside down and shake it a little, then hold it vertically while running a finger along the icing to remove the excess. Next, run a finger around the edge of the icing to make a clean edge, except in the case of a clear caramel.

FOR AN ULTRA-SMOOTH FINISH

For a finish that's nice and even, you can fill and ice éclairs upside down: pierce the top of the pastry rather than the base, fill, then ice the base, which is smooth and flat, and serve them wrong side up, icing on top.

SPECIAL ÉCLAIR ICING

USING A SPATULA

Often, the container holding the icing is too small to dip an éclair in lengthways. In this case, use a spatula, but only to transfer a generous quantity of icing to the éclair, not to spread it. The spatula mustn't touch the éclair, just deposit the icing on top. Then, even out the thickness and shape of the icing with your finger.

USING A PIPING BAG

You can also place the icing in a bag fitted with a "ribbon" nozzle (flat with small teeth) and use this to apply an even layer of icing all along the éclair.

1. Fondant with the right consistency: neither too thick, nor too runny (it falls back from being lifted up without immediately merging with the rest).

2. Fondant that's too runny, which won't give a perfect finish.

3. Dipping the choux into the icing.

STANDARD ICINGS

GANACHE / FONDANT ICING / ROYAL ICING

DARK CHOCOLATE

100 g (3½ oz) dark chocolate
120 g (4 oz) pouring (whipping) cream
1 or 2 drops of red food colouring (optional)

COFFEE

100 g (3½ oz) white chocolate
35 g (1¼ oz) pouring (whipping) cream
1 teaspoon coffee essence

GANACHE BASE

Place the chocolate, broken into pieces, into a heat-resistant bowl. Stir the cream (and the coffee essence, for the coffee ganache) in a small saucepan and heat to just below boiling point. Remove from the heat and pour the cream over the chocolate. Gently combine with a flexible spatula until the chocolate has melted. If it doesn't melt completely, pour 1 cm (½ inch) water into the saucepan, bring to the boil, turn off the heat and place the bowl on top. Mix until the ganache is nice and smooth. Incorporate the red food colouring, if desired, for the chocolate ganache.

200 g (7 oz) white fondant icing, ready-made

CHOCOLATE

50 g (1¼ oz) dark chocolate, melted
1 teaspoon honey
1 or 2 drops of red food colouring (optional)

COFFEE

2 teaspoons coffee essence
1 or 2 drops of yellow food colouring (optional)

FONDANT BASE

Heat the fondant icing to lukewarm very gently in a saucepan with a few drops of water, stirring at the same time. When the mixture is a little below body temperature (about 35°C/95°F), add the melted chocolate and the honey for the chocolate icing, or else the coffee essence for the coffee icing. Add the food colouring, if desired, then a little water until you have a mixture that falls off the spatula when it is lifted up without merging immediately with the rest of the fondant in the saucepan.
Important note: always stir the fondant before dipping a pastry into it. In effect, a thin film forms on the surface of the fondant as soon as you stop mixing it; it prevents the fondant from adhering well to the pastry and reduces its gloss.

TIPS:

Use ganache for a chocolate-coloured icing, caramel (see page 50) for a caramel-coloured icing and fondant or royal icing for all other colours. These icings vary in:
• their look: fondant icing gives a finish that stays shiny longer (the two others go matte as they dry);
• their colour: since the base colour of the white chocolate ganache is off-white, it won't be as bright when coloured as a fondant or royal icing, whose base colour is white;
• their taste: fondant and royal icing just have a sweet taste, those with a ganache base have a chocolate flavour.

100 g (3½ oz) icing
(confectioners') sugar
½ egg white
a few drops of lemon juice

CHOCOLATE

25 g (1 oz) dark chocolate, melted
1 teaspoon honey
1 or 2 drops of red food colouring
(optional)

COFFEE

1 teaspoon coffee essence
1 or 2 drops of yellow food
colouring (optional)

ROYAL ICING BASE

Mix the sugar and egg white together in a bowl with a spatula until you have a white cream. Add the lemon juice until you have a consistency that's fluid but not too runny, close to the consistency of a fondant icing: when it is lifted with a spatula, the royal icing should fall back without merging immediately with the rest of the mixture.

To make the chocolate royal icing, incorporate the melted chocolate and honey, instead of the lemon juice. Add the food colouring, once the icing is at the correct consistency.

To make the coffee royal icing, incorporate the coffee essence, instead of the lemon juice. Add the food colouring once the icing is at the correct consistency.

chocolate ganache   coffee ganache

chocolate fondant   coffee fondant

chocolate royal icing   coffee royal icing

CARAMEL

LOVELY AND CRUNCHY

150 g (5½ oz/ ⅔ cup) caster
(superfine) sugar
50 g (1¼ oz) water

TIMING

Make the caramel after the choux pastries are filled, not before: you need the caramel to be liquid to ice the éclairs correctly, and it will harden when it cools.

HOW TO MAKE CLASSIC CARAMEL

USING WATER

Pour the water, then the sugar, into a small, heavy-based saucepan (the saucepan needs to be sturdy to withstand the very high temperatures the caramel reaches, and it will distribute the heat better if it has a thick base). Wait for the sugar to absorb the water (a few seconds) and stir over medium heat until the sugar dissolves. Bring to the boil over high heat. Don't touch the sugar from this point onwards, otherwise it could crystallise. Covering the saucepan during cooking avoids crystallisation, but you mustn't forget to keep an eye on what is happening under the lid!

WITHOUT WATER

Pour the sugar (no water) into a saucepan in a layer that's not too thick and place over high heat. When part of the sugar starts to caramelise, stir constantly until all of the sugar has caramelised. This method allows you to stir the sugar because, since it is made without water, the sugar turns directly into caramel and doesn't run the risk of crystallising.

WHEN TO STOP THE CARAMELISATION

If you have a thermometer, heat the sugar to about 160°C (320°F). Otherwise, remove from the heat when the caramel has taken on a beautiful golden colour, not too dark, as it will continue to darken off the heat. Removing the caramel from the heat a little early avoids you having to stop the caramelisation process by dipping the base of the saucepan into cold water; this is preferable because when that method is used, it thickens the caramel and it becomes difficult to apply a thin layer to the éclair.

KEEP THE CARAMEL HOT

Once the caramel stops bubbling, place half the saucepan base on a cloth or an oven mitt to tilt it: that way you increase the depth of the hot mass of caramel, which makes it stay hotter longer and also makes it easier to dip the éclair into it.

WHAT IF THE CARAMEL GOES HARD?

If the caramel goes hard, reheat it and, as soon as a few small bubbles appear on the surface, remove the saucepan from the heat. If you allow the caramel to heat longer, it will brown further and the caramel will become bitter. Also, your éclairs won't all be the same colour if the caramel browns further.

FANCY ICINGS

ANYTHING IS POSSIBLE!

white icing base:
(white chocolate ganache,
fondant or royal icing:
see pages 48–49)
liquid food colouring

COLOURED ICING

Here are a few tips for colouring a white icing base. A few drops of food colouring will be enough; adjust the quantity according to the desired shade.
• To make a green icing, you need to combine equal quantities of yellow and blue. For pistachio green, you need four times more yellow than blue.
• For pink, you just need to add a very small amount of red.
• For orange, you need three times more yellow than red.
• For violet, you need one and a half times more red than blue.
• For a chestnut brown, you need equal quantities of red and yellow and three times less blue.

FOR 6 TO 8 ÉCLAIRS
100 g (3½ oz) pouring
(whipping) cream
30 g (1 oz) water
100 g (3½ oz) sugar
15 g (½ oz) salted butter

SALTED-BUTTER CARAMEL (FLOWING ICING)

Scald the cream (heat until just below boiling point) in a small saucepan and set aside.

Pour the water, then the sugar, into a small heavy-based saucepan. Wait for the sugar to absorb the water (a few seconds), then cover and bring to the boil, not touching the saucepan. Allow the caramel to colour, checking it from time to time.

When the caramel has reached a lovely mahogany colour (reddish-brown), remove the saucepan from the heat, add the hot cream all at once and combine with a spatula. If the mixture isn't perfectly smooth, place it over medium heat for 2 minutes, while stirring. Add the salted butter in small pieces off the heat. Mix well.

FOR 6 TO 8 ÉCLAIRS
200 g (7 oz) dark chocolate
2 teaspoons neutral-flavoured
oil (such as peanut, grapeseed
or sunflower)
icing (confectioners') sugar, to
dust (optional)

CHOCOLATE SHELL

Place the choux pastries in the freezer for about 20 minutes: it must be very cold but not necessarily frozen.

Melt the chocolate over low heat with the oil and combine. Once it is smooth and warm, take the choux pastries out of the freezer and place them on a wire rack positioned on top of a sheet of baking paper. Pour the hot chocolate over the cold éclairs in a swift motion. Make sure the pastries are well covered with chocolate. Wait for a few moments for the chocolate to set. If there's not enough chocolate, scrape up the chocolate that has fallen onto the baking paper with a flexible spatula and reheat it in the saucepan, then pour it on the éclairs.

Remove the pastries from the rack carefully one by one, with the help of a small spatula, and serve on plates. Dust with icing sugar, if desired.

Clockwise from top left: two-tone icing; speckled effect;
millefeuille style; instant topping.

CUSTOMISATION
FANCY HATS FOR YOUR CHOUX

TWO-TONE ICING USING A SPOON

Make a bowl of icing in a different colour from the one that's already on the choux. The icing that's already on the choux must be dry, and the icing that you're applying should be quite liquid. Dip the spoon into the icing, lift it out and allow the excess to fall into the bowl. When the icing runs thinly off the spoon, draw shapes on the choux.

SPECKLED EFFECT

Dip a kitchen or pastry brush into some food colouring and run your finger along the top of the brush so you spray small drops onto the icing. The latter must be dry, otherwise the drops will be diluted in the icing.

INSTANT TOPPING

When the choux buns have just been iced, dip their tops into chocolate sprinkles or shredded coconut. Press lightly and set the choux back upright.

MILLE FEUILLE-STYLE

Ice the choux with white fondant. Without delay, make lines of melted chocolate or chocolate fondant across the icing using a spoon (the chocolate fondant will stay shiny while the melted chocolate will become matte). Drag a toothpick across the lines to make a zigzag pattern.

MISCELLANEOUS DECORATIONS

To customise your choux pastries, you can also use gold or silver leaf, silver cachous, coloured sugar, icing (confectioners') sugar, and crushed Gavotte (crêpe dentelle) biscuits or brandy snaps, organic flower petals (roses, pansies, violets). To help these decorations stick to a dry icing, lightly moisten your finger and run it over the spot you're decorating before applying the selected decorations.

FAQ

DO I NEED TO HAVE NOZZLES IN ALL THE DIFFERENT SIZES?

No. Nozzle sizes generally range between 2 and 20 mm, their diameter increasing by one millimetre at a time. Within this range, you will need at least one medium-sized plain nozzle and one large plain nozzle. If you already have some nozzles at home that are just a little smaller or a little larger than those recommended in this book, they will be perfectly fine. A difference of 2 mm will be almost unnoticeable. Star nozzles are used for decorations, so they are more a matter of choice and can be replaced with plain nozzles. If, however, you would like to improve the presentation of your éclairs, have on hand at least one medium-sized star nozzle and one large one (between 14 and 16 mm).

WHY DO MY CHOUX PASTRIES SOMETIMES NOT PUFF UP?

Two possibilities: the pastry dough is too liquid as a result of too many eggs being added, or the oven door was opened before the choux pastries had time to puff up. Sometimes choux pastry puffs up and then collapses: it can also be because the oven door was opened before their internal structure (formed by the egg and flour, see "What makes choux pastry puff up?") has stabilised.

WHY DO MY CHOUX PASTRIES SOMETIMES COLLAPSE WHEN I TAKE THEM OUT OF THE OVEN AND/OR HAVE AN "EGGY" TASTE?

Because they aren't cooked enough. In pastry making, items are often taken out of the oven as soon as they are puffed up and brown. If you do this with choux pastry, the choux will collapse, the inside will be pasty and have an omelette-like taste. You need to wait much longer before taking choux pastry out of the oven. This is, moreover, the advantage of the recipe given in this book, which recommends cooking the choux pastry in a moderately slow oven (150°C/300°F/Gas 2): there is thus little risk of overcooking the pastry, which has all the time it needs to get a good puff and colour before being taken out of the oven.

Tip: choux pastry is cooked once the furrows resulting from the crackling are as coloured as the rest of the surface.

HOW CAN I AVOID LUMPS IN MY CHOUX PASTRY DOUGH?

The liquid mixture of water, milk and melted butter must be brought to a full boil before the flour is added off the heat. A full boil means that large bubbles should appear across the whole surface of the liquid and, once these bubbles have formed, you need to wait 2 or 3 seconds before taking the saucepan off the heat. That's the moment the flour needs to be added, all at once. If you add the flour before the liquid is hot enough, small grains will appear in the pastry dough. Don't worry if this happens, as these won't make much of a difference to the final result.

WHAT MAKES CHOUX PASTRY PUFF UP?

Like flaky pastry, choux pastry puffs up during cooking without the addition of any raising agent or egg whites. The explanation is as follows: choux pastry dough contains a lot of liquid (the water and the liquid contained in the eggs and in the milk). It is in some ways a very thick liquid. In the oven, under the action of the heat, the choux pastry blisters and boils, releasing a lot of steam. At the same time, the air that was trapped in the mixture when the eggs were added expands. These two phenomena lead to the puffing of the choux pastry. The steam will crackle the outer shell of the choux pastry to escape, then the flour and egg will thicken and coagulate into a solid structure, which will support the fully formed pastry.

WHY DO I NEED TO USE PLAIN (ALL-PURPOSE) FLOUR AND NOT A STRONGER VARIETY?

Because plain flour (the flour most commonly used in pâtisserie) contains less gluten. When gluten comes into contact with water and is kneaded, it forms a network of proteins that becomes denser the longer the dough is worked. This network is necessary, because it allows the pastry to puff up and hold together, but the denser the network, the heavier the pastry will become and the more it will shrink as it cooks. Choux pastry is worked quite a lot: it is mixed vigorously as the egg is incorporated. This is why a gluten-rich flour produces choux pastries that are tough and mis-shapen.

Recipes

COFFEE OR CHOCOLATE ÉCLAIRS

80 ml (2½ fl oz/⅓ cup)
full-cream milk
80 ml (2½ fl oz/⅓ cup) water
70 g (2½ oz) butter
large pinch of salt
10 g (¼ oz) sugar
100 g (3½ oz/⅔ cup) plain
(all-purpose) flour
2 eggs

THE ÉCLAIRS

Make a slightly drier choux pastry dough (see pages 24–27) so your éclairs will be nice and straight; to do this, stop adding egg when the mixture clings to the spatula and only falls off after a long pause. Use it to fill a piping bag fitted with a plain 20 mm nozzle. Position it at a 45 degree angle in relation to the baking tray and push out the mixture while moving the bag in one clean movement so the éclair has a nice straight shape; place an even pressure on the bag so that the tube of mixture that comes out has the same diameter as the nozzle. Once the éclair is 14 cm (5½ in) long, cut off the mixture with a smooth-bladed knife. If required, smooth the éclairs (using your finger) with some of the beaten egg left over from making the mixture, or else with water. Bake at 150°C (300°F/Gas 2) for 55–60 minutes. Remove from the tray, allow to cool.

CHOCOLATE CRÈME PÂTISSIÈRE

55 g (2 oz) pouring (whipping) cream
65 g (2¼ oz) dark chocolate (50–60% cocoa)
165 g (5 ¾ oz) full-cream milk
35 g (1¼ oz) sugar
2 egg yolks
½ pinch of salt
8 g (³⁄₁₆ oz) plain (all-purpose) flour
8 g (³⁄₁₆ oz) cornflour

THE CRÈME PÂTISSIÈRE

CHOCOLATE – Scald the cream (heat until just below boiling point) in a small saucepan and pour it over the chocolate broken up into pieces. Stir to make a thick ganache. Make a plain crème pâtissière (see page 32) using remaining ingredients and combine it while it is still warm with the ganache.
COFFEE – Make a plain crème pâtissière (see page 32) using all of the ingredients except for the coffee essence. At the end of the cooking, whisk in the coffee essence.

ASSEMBLY

Pierce the base of the éclairs, making three holes using a 6 mm nozzle or with the tip of a ballpoint pen. Fill a piping bag fitted with a plain 8 mm nozzle with crème pâtissière and start to fill the éclairs from one of the ends. When the crème appears in the middle hole, finish filling from the other end. Stop when the crème comes out the two other holes.

COFFEE CRÈME PÂTISSIÈRE

250 g (9 oz) full-cream milk
50 g (1¼ oz) sugar
3 egg yolks
pinch of salt
10 g (¼ oz) plain (all-purpose) flour
10 g (¼ oz) cornflour (cornstarch)
2–3 teaspoons coffee essence

continued >

> continued from previous page

THE ICING

125 g (4½ oz) dark chocolate cocoa
50 g (1¼ oz) butter
40 g (1½ oz) honey
125 g (4½ oz) pouring (whipping) cream

CHOCOLATE – Place the chocolate, broken up into pieces, the butter, diced, and the honey into a heatproof bowl, that's large enough to contain an éclair. Scald the cream in a saucepan, remove from the heat and pour into the bowl over the chocolate. Combine with a flexible spatula. If the mixture isn't completely melted, pour 1 cm (½ inch) water into the saucepan used for the cream and bring to the boil, then remove from the heat. Place the bowl on top and stir until the ganache is smooth. Without further delay, remove the bowl from the saucepan, dip the top of the éclairs into the ganache and keep in the refrigerator until ready to use.

300 g (10½ oz) white fondant icing, ready-made
2 to 3 teaspoons coffee essence
yellow food colouring (optional)

COFFEE – Heat the fondant icing and a few drops of water to lukewarm in a saucepan (that's large enough to contain an eclair) over very low heat, stirring. Once the mixture is a little below body temperature (about 35°C/95°F), incorporate the coffee essence and add some lukewarm water just until you have a mixture that, when it is lifted up, falls back without immediately merging into the rest of the icing in the saucepan. Add the food colouring, if using, and remove from the heat. Dip the top side of the éclairs in the icing, then hold them vertically above the saucepan and remove the excess icing with a finger. Next, run your finger around the icing so you have a clean edge.

EARL GREY, WHITE CHOCOLATE OR CHOC-MINT ÉCLAIRS

6 to 8 éclairs (see pages 24–29)
ingredients for double quantity
dark chocolate ganache
(see page 48)
5 g (⅛ oz) Earl Grey tea leaves

CRÈME PÂTISSIÈRE
325 ml (11 fl oz) full-cream milk
4 egg yolks
65 g (2¼ oz) sugar
15 g (½ oz) plain (all-purpose)
flour
15 g (½ oz) cornflour
(cornstarch)
pinch of salt

6 to 8 éclairs (see pages 24–29)
50 ml (1½ fl oz) pouring
(whipping) cream
130 g (4¾ oz) white chocolate
ingredients for crème
pâtissière (above)
white chocolate ganache (see
page 44), extra, for icing
white chocolate shavings,
to decorate

6 to 8 éclairs (see pages 24–29)
double quantity dark
chocolate ganache
(see page 48)
1 bunch fresh mint
ingredients for crème pâtissière
(above)
mint-flavoured sweets or
sprinkles, to decorate

EARL GREY FILLING

Scald the cream and pour it over the chocolate, broken into pieces, then stir until you have a thick ganache. Place the tea leaves in the saucepan with the milk. Bring to the boil, then remove from the heat, cover and allow to infuse for 5–10 minutes. Strain the milk, pressing down on the tea. Make the crème pâtissière (see page 32) using this infused milk. While the crème pâtissière is still warm, combine it with half of the ganache. Cover with plastic wrap placed in direct contact with the crème to prevent it forming a skin and keep in the refrigerator until ready to use.

Fill each éclair with the flavoured crème pâtissière (see page 30) and ice with the remaining chocolate ganache. If desired, drizzle a small amount of ganache icing from a spoon to write 'Earl Grey' on top.

WHITE CHOCOLATE FILLING

Scald the cream and pour it over the chocolate, broken into pieces. Place the bowl containing the chocolate over the saucepan used to heat the cream: the residual heat will give off a little warmth and help the chocolate to melt. Stir until you have a thick ganache. Make a plain crème pâtissière (see page 32) and, while it is still warm, combine with the ganache. Cover with plastic wrap placed in direct contact with the crème and keep in the refrigerator until ready to use.

Fill each éclair with the flavoured crème pâtissière (see page 30) and decorate with white chocolate icing. Sprinkle white chocolate shavings generously over the top to decorate.

CHOC-MINT FILLING

Scald the cream and pour it over the chocolate, broken into pieces, then stir until you have a thick ganache. Wash and dry the bunch of mint. Pour the milk into a saucepan, add the mint and bring to the boil. Discard the mint and make the crème pâtissière (see page 32) using this infused milk. While the crème pâtissière is still warm, combine it with half of the ganache. Cover with plastic wrap placed in direct contact with the crème and keep in the refrigerator until ready to use.

Fill each éclair with the flavoured crème pâtissière (see page 30) and ice with the remaining chocolate ganache. Decorate with mint-flavoured sprinkles or sweets as desired.

DOUBLE COFFEE OR MOCHA ÉCLAIRS

6 to 8 éclairs (see pages 24–29)
100 g (3½ oz) butter
250 g (9 oz) dark chocolate
(50–70% cocoa)
2 teaspoons coffee essence
6 egg whites
40 g (1½ oz) caster (superfine)
sugar
large pinch of salt
4 egg yolks
coffee fondant icing (see page 48)

MOCHA MOUSSE FILLING

Place the butter, in small dices, in a small saucepan over low heat and the chocolate, broken into pieces, on top. Once the butter has melted, submerge the chocolate in the butter. Wait a few moments and combine until the mixture is smooth, then add the coffee essence, stir and remove from the heat.

Whisk the egg whites to firm peaks. Add the sugar and salt, and continue whisking. Add a third of the chocolate mixture to the egg yolks and mix well with a whisk. Incorporate the second third, then the remaining third. Add a quarter of the whisked egg whites to the chocolate mixture and whisk, then incorporate the remaining egg whites in three stages, folding them in gently with a flexible spatula. Allow to set in the refrigerator for 2 hours.

Slice each éclair in half lengthways and fill the bottom half with the choc –coffee mousse (see page 30). Ice the top with coffee fondant icing (see page 46) and assemble the éclair.

6 to 8 éclairs (see pages 24–29)
250 ml (9 fl oz/1 cup) full-cream
milk
3 egg yolks
50 g (1¾ oz) sugar
10 g (¼ oz) plain (all-purpose)
flour
10 g (¼ oz) cornflour
(cornstarch)
pinch of salt
2 teaspoons coffee essence
120 g (4¼ oz) softened butter
coffee fondant icing (see page 48)

COFFEE CRÈME MOUSSELINE FILLING

Make a plain crème pâtissière (see page 32) using all the ingredients, except the coffee essence, butter and icing. Add the coffee essence and cool the crème by whisking until it has the consistency of mayonnaise. Whisk the butter until it has the same consistency. For the two mixtures to combine properly, they need to have the same consistency but not the same temperature: the crème pâtissière must be cold and the butter lukewarm. Add the softened butter to the crème, then whisk until you have a light cream. Place plastic wrap in direct contact with the crème mousseline to prevent it forming a skin and keep in the refrigerator until ready to use.

Fill each éclair with the coffee crème mousseline (see page 30) and ice with the coffee fondant icing (see page 46).

VANILLA ÉCLAIRS

1 vanilla bean
410 ml (14¼ fl oz) full-cream milk
80 g (2¼ oz) sugar
5 egg yolks
20 g (¾ oz) plain (all-purpose) flour
20 g (¾ oz) cornflour (cornstarch)
large pinch of salt

VANILLA CRÈME PÂTISSIÈRE

Split the vanilla bean and scrape out the seeds. Add the seeds, as well as the bean, to the milk with half the sugar. Bring to the boil then remove from the heat. Cover and allow to infuse for 5–10 minutes. Make the crème pâtissière (see page 32) with this infused milk, removing the bean from the milk before mixing with the egg yolks.

80 ml (2½ fl oz/⅓ cup) milk
80 ml (2½ fl oz/⅓ cup) water
70 g (2½ oz) butter
large pinch of salt
10 g (¼ oz) sugar
100 g (3½ oz/⅔ cup) plain (all-purpose) flour
2 eggs

THE ÉCLAIRS

Preheat the oven to 150°C (300°F/Gas 2). Make the choux pastry dough and pipe the éclairs onto a baking tray (see pages 24–29). Place in the oven and cook for 55–60 minutes. Remove from the oven and allow to cool on a wire rack.

1 teaspoon rum, Grand Marnier or calvados (optional)

ASSEMBLY

Whisk the cooled crème pâtissière vigorously with the alcohol, if desired, until it becomes soft, smooth and creamy again. Pierce three holes in the base of each éclair. Fill a piping bag fitted with a plain 8 mm nozzle with crème pâtissière. Start filling the éclairs from one of the ends; when the crème appears in the middle hole, continue filling from the other end. Stop when the crème comes out of the other two holes and the éclairs are nice and heavy. Wipe them against the edge of a bowl to remove the excess crème.

300 g (10½ oz) white fondant icing, ready-made
1 teaspoon natural vanilla extract and/or
1 pinch of ground vanilla

THE VANILLA ICING: VANILLA-FLAVOURED FONDANT

Heat the fondant and a few drops of water to lukewarm in a saucepan set over very low heat, stirring. When the mixture is a little below body temperature (about 35°C/95°F), incorporate the natural vanilla extract and/or ground vanilla and add some lukewarm water until you have an icing that doesn't immediately merge with the rest of the mixture in the saucepan when it is lifted up and dropped. Dip the top side of the éclairs in the icing, then hold them vertically above the saucepan and remove the excess with a finger. Then, run a finger around the icing to make a clean edge.

CHESTNUT ÉCLAIRS

80 ml (2½ fl oz/⅓ cup) milk
80 ml (2½ fl oz/⅓ cup) water
70 g (2½ oz) butter
large pinch of salt
10 g (¼ oz) sugar
100 g (3½ oz/⅔ cup) plain
(all-purpose) flour
2 eggs

THE ÉCLAIRS

Preheat the oven to 150°C (300°F/Gas 2). Make the choux pastry dough (see pages 24–27) and use it to fill a piping bag fitted with a plain 20 mm nozzle. Position the nozzle at a 45 degree angle in relation to the baking tray and push out the mixture while moving the piping bag along in one clean movement to give the éclair a nice straight shape; apply an even pressure to the bag so that the tube of mixture that comes out has the same diameter as the nozzle. When the éclair is 14 cm (5½ inches) long, cut off the mixture with a smooth-bladed knife. If necessary, smooth the éclairs with some beaten egg left over from making the pastry or else with water. Bake for 55 – 60 minutes. Remove from the oven and allow to cool on a wire rack.

4 egg yolks
8 g (³⁄₁₆ oz) cornflour
(cornstarch)
100 ml (3½ fl oz) full-cream
milk
230 g (8 oz) crème de marrons
(sweetened chestnut purée)
120 g (4¼ oz) butter, diced
1 teaspoon rum

THE CHESTNUT CRÈME PÂTISSIÈRE

Combine the egg yolks with the cornflour. Heat the milk to lukewarm in a small saucepan, then remove from the heat and incorporate the crème de marrons with a whisk. Return to the heat and bring to the boil. Add the mixture to the egg yolks, whisk vigorously and allow to boil for 1–2 minutes.

Remove from the heat and incorporate the butter in pieces, then the rum. Transfer to a bowl, cover with plastic wrap in direct contact with the crème to prevent it forming a skin and refrigerate.

ASSEMBLY

Once the éclairs have cooled, slice them in half lengthways using a serrated knife. Fill a piping bag fitted with a plain 12 mm nozzle with the crème pâtissière (or use a spoon) and fill the bottom half of each éclair generously. Place the top halves of the éclairs on top and press very lightly. Keep in the refrigerator.

50 g (1¾ oz) crème de marrons

THE ICING (optional)

Gently spread a little crème de marrons on the éclairs.

NUTELLA® ÉCLAIRS

80 ml (2½ fl oz/⅓ cup) milk
80 ml (2½ fl oz/⅓ cup) water
70 g (2½ oz) butter
large pinch of salt
10 g (¼ oz) sugar
100 g (3½ oz/⅔ cup) plain
(all-purpose) flour
2 eggs

THE ÉCLAIRS
Preheat the oven to 150°C (300°F/Gas 2). Make the choux pastry dough
(see pages 24–27) and use it to fill a piping bag fitted with a plain 20 mm
nozzle. Position the nozzle at a 45 degree angle in relation to the baking
tray and push out the mixture while moving the piping bag along in one
clean movement to give the éclair a nice straight shape; apply an even
pressure to the bag so that the tube of mixture that comes out has the
same diameter as the nozzle. When the éclair is 14 cm (5½ inches) long,
cut off the mixture with a smooth-bladed knife. If necessary, smooth the
éclairs with some beaten egg left over from making the pastry or else with
water. Bake for 55–60 minutes. Remove from the oven and allow to cool
on a wire rack.

325 ml (11 fl oz) full-cream
milk
4 egg yolks
65 g (2¼ oz) sugar
15 g (½ oz) plain (all-purpose)
flour
15 g (½ oz) cornflour
(cornstarch)
pinch of salt
140 g (5 oz) Nutella®

NUTELLA® CRÈME PÂTISSIÈRE
Make a plain crème pâtissière (see page 32) using all the ingredients
except the Nutella®. When cool, add the Nutella® and combine.

ASSEMBLY
Once the éclairs have cooled, slice them in half lengthways using a
serrated knife. Fill a piping bag fitted with a plain 12 mm nozzle with
the Nutella® crème pâtissière (or use a spoon) and fill the bottom half
of each éclair generously. Place the top halves of the éclairs on top
and press very lightly. Keep in the refrigerator.

50 g (1¾ oz) Nutella®

THE ICING (optional)
Gently spread a little Nutella® on the éclairs.

CRUNCHY HAZELNUT ÉCLAIRS

325 ml (11 fl oz) full-cream milk
4 egg yolks
65 g (2¼ oz) sugar
15 g (½ oz) plain (all-purpose) flour
15 g (½ oz) cornflour (cornstarch)
pinch of salt
150 g (5½ oz) hazelnuts

HAZELNUT CRÈME PÂTISSIÈRE

Preheat oven to 160°C (315°F/Gas 2–3). Make a plain crème pâtissière (see page 32) using all the ingredients except the hazelnuts. Cover with plastic wrap placed in direct contact with the crème to prevent it forming a skin and refrigerate it. Spread the hazelnuts on a baking tray. Bake for about 30 minutes: they should be very brown, almost black. Allow to cool and set 50 g (1¾ oz/⅓ cup) aside for decorating. Crush the rest. Mix them into the cooled crème, whisking vigorously. Re-cover the crème and keep it in the refrigerator until ready to use.

80 ml (2½ fl oz/⅓ cup) milk
80 ml (2½ fl oz/⅓ cup) water
70 g (2½ oz) butter
large pinch of salt
10 g (¼ oz) sugar
100 g (3½ oz/⅔ cup) plain (all-purpose) flour
2 eggs

THE ÉCLAIRS

Preheat the oven to 150°C (300°F/Gas 2). Make the choux pastry dough (see pages 24–27) and use this to fill a piping bag fitted with a plain 20 mm nozzle. Position at a 45 degree angle in relation to the baking tray and push out the mixture while moving the bag in one clean movement to give the éclair a nice straight shape; apply an even pressure to piping bag so that the tube of mixture that comes out has the same diameter as the nozzle. When the éclair is 14 cm (5½ inches) long, cut off the mixture with a smooth-bladed knife. If necessary, smooth the éclairs with some of the beaten egg left over from making the pastry or else with water. Bake for 55–60 minutes. Remove from the oven and allow to cool on a wire rack.

ASSEMBLY

Once the éclairs have cooled, fill them with the hazelnut crème pâtissière (see page 30).

300 g (10½ oz) white fondant icing, ready-made

THE ICING: FONDANT + HAZELNUT PIECES

Chop the reserved roasted hazelnuts into small pieces. Heat the fondant icing with a few drops of water over a very low heat, stirring. When the mixture is (a little below body temperature) about 35°C/95°F, add some lukewarm water until you have an icing that drops from the spatula without merging immediately with the rest of the fondant. Remove from the heat. Dip the top of an éclair into the icing, then hold it vertically and run a finger over it to remove the excess icing. Run a finger around the edge of the icing so you have a nice clean edge and arrange the pieces of hazelnut on top straight away. Ice and decorate the other éclairs in the same way, taking care to stir the fondant well before each dipping.

FRANGIPANE ÉCLAIRS

170 ml (5½ fl oz/⅔ cup) full-cream milk
2 egg yolks
35 g (1¼ oz) sugar
8 g (³⁄₁₆ oz) plain (all-purpose) flour
8 g (³⁄₁₆ oz) cornflour (cornstarch)
½ pinch of salt
155 g (5½ oz) ground almonds, sifted
155 g (5½ oz) softened butter
155 g (5½ oz) icing sugar, sifted
1 teaspoon natural vanilla extract
1 teaspoon dark rum

THE FRANGIPANE

Make a plain crème pâtissière (see page 32), cover with plasitc wrap placed in direct contact with the crème to prevent it forming a skin and refrigerate.

Next make an almond cream. Preheat the oven to 160°C (315°F/Gas 2–3) and toast the ground almonds for 10 minutes on a tray. Allow to cool. Combine the softened butter with 2 tablespoons of icing sugar until the mixture is smooth. Add the rest of the icing sugar, the ground almonds, vanilla extract and rum.

Whisk the crème pâtissière until it is smooth and mix it into the almond cream. Cover with plastic wrap in direct contact with the frangipane and keep in the refrigerator until ready to use.

80 ml (2½ fl oz/⅓ cup) milk
80 ml (2½ fl oz/⅓ cup) water
70 g (2½ oz) butter
large pinch of salt
10 g (¼ oz) sugar
100 g (3½ oz/⅔ cup) plain (all-purpose) flour
2 eggs
120 g (4¼ oz/1¼ cup) flaked almonds
icing sugar

THE ÉCLAIRS

Preheat oven to 150°C (300°F/Gas 2). Make the choux pastry dough (see pages 24–27) and use it to fill a piping bag fitted with a plain 20 mm nozzle. Position it at a 45 degree angle in relation to the baking tray and push out the mixture while moving the bag in one clean movement to give the éclair a nice straight shape; apply an even pressure to the piping bag so that the tube of mixture that comes out has the same diameter as the nozzle. When the éclair is 14 cm (5½ inches) long, cut off the mixture with a smooth-bladed knife. Smooth the shape using a finger or brush with beaten egg or water to give a regular shape to the éclairs and so that the almonds will stick. Cover éclairs generously with flaked almonds, then tip up the tray to allow the excess to fall off. Bake for 55–60 minutes. Remove from oven and allow to cool on a wire rack.

ASSEMBLY

When the éclairs are cool, slice them in half lengthways using a serrated knife. Fill a piping bag fitted with a plain 12 mm nozzle with the frangipane and fill the bottom half of each éclair generously. Place the top half back on, pressing very lightly. Dust the éclairs with icing sugar just before serving.

LIME ÉCLAIRS

1 lime
410 ml (14¼ fl oz) full-cream milk
5 egg yolks
80 g (2¼ oz) sugar
20 g (¼ oz) plain (all-purpose) flour
20 g (¾ oz) cornflour (cornstarch)
large pinch of salt

CHOUX PASTRY
80 ml (2½ fl oz/⅓ cup) milk
80 ml (2½ fl oz/⅓ cup) water
70 g (2½ oz) butter
large pinch of salt
10 g (¼ oz) sugar
100 g (3½ oz/⅔ cup) plain (all-purpose) flour
2 eggs

1 lime
300 g (10½ oz) white fondant icing, ready-made
yellow and blue food colouring (optional)

THE LIME CRÈME PÂTISSIÈRE

Wash the lime, remove the zest and reserve the fruit. Add the zest to the milk and make a crème pâtissière with this infused milk (see page 32). Cover with plastic wrap placed in direct contact with the crème to prevent it forming a skin and refrigerate.

THE ÉCLAIRS

Preheat the oven to 150°C (300°F/Gas 2). Make the choux pastry dough (see pages 24–27) and use it to fill a piping bag fitted with a plain 20 mm nozzle. Position it at a 45 degree angle in relation to the baking tray and push out the mixture while moving the bag in one clean movement to give the éclair a nice straight shape; apply an even pressure to the piping bag so that the tube of mixture that comes out has the same diameter as the nozzle. When the éclair is 14 cm (5½ inches) long, cut off the mixture with a smooth-bladed knife. If necessary, smooth the éclairs with some of the beaten egg left over from making the pastry or else with water. Bake for 55–60 minutes. Remove from the oven and allow to cool on a wire rack.

ASSEMBLY

Juice the reserved lime, add half of the juice to the cooled crème pâtissière and whisk vigorously until smooth. Taste and add more lime juice if desired, then fill the éclairs with lime crème pâtissière (see page 30).

THE ICING: FONDANT + ZEST

Zest the lime and reserve. Warm the fondant over very low heat to lukewarm with a few drops of water, stirring constantly. When the mixture is a little below body temperature (about 35°C/ 95°F), add a little more lukewarm water until you have an icing that drops from the spatula without merging immediately with the rest of the fondant. Add the yellow and blue food colouring, if desired, until you have a pretty lime green then remove from the heat.

Dip the top of a filled éclair in the icing, then hold it vertically and run a finger over it to remove the excess icing. Run a finger around the edge of the icing so you have a nice clean edge. Scatter the top with lime zest. Ice and decorate the other éclairs in the same way, making sure you stir the fondant well before each use.

CHOC-ORANGE ÉCLAIRS

ORANGE CRÈME PÂTISSIÈRE

1 orange
410 ml (14¼ fl oz) full-cream milk
5 egg yolks
80 g (2¾ oz) sugar
20 g (¾ oz) plain (all-purpose) flour
20 g (¾ oz) cornflour
large pinch of salt

CHOUX PASTRY

80 ml (2½ fl oz/⅓ cup) milk
80 ml (2½ fl oz/⅓ cup) water
70 g (2½ oz) butter
large pinch of salt
10 g (¼ oz) sugar
100 g (3½ oz/⅔ cup) plain (all-purpose) flour
2 eggs

CHOCOLATE SHELL

250 g (9 oz) dark chocolate (50–70% cocoa)
2 teaspoons neutral-flavoured oil (peanut, grapeseed or sunflower)
candied orange zest

ORANGE–CHOC ICING

250 g (9 oz) orange-coloured fondant icing (see page 52)
chocolate sprinkles or
50 g (1¾ oz) dark chocolate, melted

THE ORANGE CRÈME PÂTISSIÈRE

Wash the orange, remove the zest and reserve the fruit. Add the zest to the milk and make a crème pâtissière with the infused milk (see page 32). Refrigerate.

THE ÉCLAIRS

Preheat oven to 150°C (300°F/Gas 2). Make choux pastry dough and pipe the mixture onto a baking tray (see pages 24–29). Bake for 55–60 minutes. Remove from the oven and allow to cool on a wire rack.

ASSEMBLY

Squeeze the reserved orange. Add half the juice to the cooled crème pâtissière and whisk vigorously until smooth. Taste and, if necessary, add a little more orange juice. Now fill the éclairs with the orange crème pâtissière (see page 30) and refrigerate.

THE ICING

Choose one of the following icing and decorating methods for each batch of 6 to 8 éclairs.

CHOCOLATE SHELL + ZEST – Place the éclairs in the freezer for 15 minutes: they should be very cold but not frozen. Melt the chocolate over low heat with the oil, then stir to make the mixture smooth. Take the éclairs out of the freezer and place them on a wire rack. Pour the warm chocolate over the cold éclairs in a rapid motion so that you cover them completely. Avoid going over the same area more than once to keep the layer of chocolate thin. Wait a few moments for the chocolate to set a little, then carefully arrange a few pieces of zest on the chocolate shell. Serve straight away or keep in the refrigerator until serving time, within a day.

ORANGE–CHOC ICING – Dip the top of a filled éclair in the icing, then hold it vertically and run a finger over it to remove the excess icing. Run a finger around the edge of the icing so you have a nice clean edge. If using chocolate sprinkles, immediately dip the éclair in the sprinkles, then ice the remaining éclairs in the same way, making sure you stir the fondant well before each use.

If using the melted chocolate for decoration, ice all of the éclairs and allow the icing to dry. Melt the chocolate in a saucepan, then use a spoon to drizzle tiger stripes across the iced éclairs.

CARAMELISED APPLE ÉCLAIRS

80 ml (2½ fl oz/⅓ cup) milk
80 ml (2½ fl oz/⅓ cup) water
70 g (2½ oz) butter
large pinch of salt
10 g (¼ oz) sugar
100 g (3½ oz/⅔ cup) plain
(all-purpose) flour
2 eggs

THE ÉCLAIRS

Preheat the oven to 150°C (300°F/Gas 2). Make the choux pastry dough (see pages 24–27) and use it to fill a piping bag fitted with a plain 20 mm nozzle. Position it at a 45 degree angle in relation to the baking tray and push out the mixture while moving the bag in one clean movement to give the éclair a nice straight shape; apply an even pressure to the piping bag so that the tube of mixture that comes out of the nozzle has the same diameter as the nozzle. When the éclair is 14 cm (5½ inches) long, cut off the mixture with a smooth-bladed knife. If necessary, smooth the éclairs with some of the beaten egg left over from making the pastry or else with water. Bake for 55–60 minutes. Remove from the oven and allow to cool.

CRÈME PÂTISSIÈRE

170 ml (5½ fl oz/⅔ cup)
full-cream milk
2 egg yolks
35 g (1¼ oz) sugar
8 g (³⁄₁₆ oz) plain (all-purpose)
flour
8 g (³⁄₁₆ oz) cornflour
½ pinch of salt
1 teaspoon calvados (optional)

LIGHT CARAMELISED APPLE CREAM

Make a plain crème pâtissière and a chantilly cream (see pages 32 and 40). Cover with plastic wrap placed in direct contact with the mixture to keep them from forming a skin and keep in the refrigerator until ready to use. Peel and core the apples then chop them into small dice. Split the vanilla bean and scrape out the seeds. Melt the butter, diced, in a saucepan over high heat. Add the vanilla seeds and bean then the sugar and, once that has melted, the diced apple. Allow them to cook, stirring carefully, until caramelised. Set aside until cooled to room temperature.
Whisk the crème pâtissière vigorously until smooth. Incorporate the chantilly cream, then add the caramelised apple and its juice. Refrigerate.

CHANTILLY CREAM

250 ml (9 fl oz/1 cup) very cold
pouring (whipping) cream
25 g (1 oz) icing sugar
1 teaspoon natural vanilla
extract
1 teaspoon calvados (optional)

ASSEMBLY

Pierce three holes in the base of the éclairs using a 6 mm nozzle or with the tip of a ballpoint pen. Fill a piping bag fitted with a plain 8 mm nozzle with the caramelised apple crème and start filling the éclairs from one of the ends. When the cream appears in the middle hole, finish filling from the other end. Stop when the cream comes out the other two holes.

CARAMELISED APPLE

2 apples
½ vanilla bean
30 g (1 oz) butter
30 g (1 oz) sugar

300 g (10½ oz) white fondant
icing, ready-made
yellow and blue food colouring
(optional)
small round sweets (optional)

THE ICING

On a very low heat, heat the fondant to lukewarm with a few drops of water, stirring constantly. When the mixture is about 35°C (95°F), add a little lukewarm water until you have a mixture that drops from the spatula without merging immediately with the rest of the fondant. Tint with the yellow and blue food colouring to a pretty green, if desired, then remove from the heat. Dip the top of an éclair into the icing, then hold it vertically and run a finger over it to remove the excess icing. Add small sweets or other decorations (see page 55 for ideas on customisation). For striped icing, only colour half of the fondant, then fill two piping bags fitted with plain 6 mm nozzles. Draw lines on the éclair, alternating the colours.

PASSIONFRUIT, MANDARIN OR STRAWBERRY ÉCLAIRS

80 ml (2½ fl oz/⅓ cup) milk
80 ml (2½ fl oz/⅓ cup) water
70 g (2½ oz) butter
large pinch of salt
10 g (¼ oz) sugar
100 g (3½ oz/⅔ cup) plain (all-purpose) flour
2 eggs

THE ÉCLAIRS

Preheat the oven to 150°C (300°F/Gas 2). Make the choux pastry (see pages 24–27) and use it to fill a piping bag fitted with a plain 20 mm nozzle. Position it at a 45 degree angle in relation to the baking tray and push out the mixture while moving the bag in one clean movement to give the éclair a nice straight shape; apply an even pressure to the piping bag so that the tube of mixture that comes out of the nozzle has the same diameter as the nozzle. When the éclair is 14 cm (5½ in) long, cut off the mixture with a smooth-bladed knife. If necessary, smooth the éclairs with some of the beaten egg left over from making the pastry or else with water. Bake for 55–60 minutes. Remove from the oven and allow to cool on a wire rack.

THE FRUIT COMPOTE

Choose one of the following compote flavours for each batch of 6 to 8 éclairs.

PASSIONFRUIT COMPOTE
10 passionfruit
70 g (2½ oz) sugar
2 g (1/16 oz) pectin

PASSIONFRUIT – Cut the passionfruit in half, empty out the pulp and strain it to collect the juice. Pour 70 g (2½ oz) of juice into a saucepan, add the sugar and the pectin. Cook over a high heat until just below boiling point, while stirring. Lower the heat and simmer gently until it thickens (5–10 minutes). Keep in the refrigerator until ready to use.

MANDARIN COMPOTE
2 clementine mandarins
65 g (2¼ oz) sugar
2 g (1/16 oz) pectin

MANDARIN – Peel the clementine mandarins, divide into segments and then cut the segments in half. Place 80 g (2¾ oz) of the mandarin segments in a saucepan, add the sugar and pectin, and stir to combine. Cook over high heat, mashing the fruit with a fork and removing the segment skins. Once the mixture is just below boiling point, lower the heat and simmer gently until it thickens (5–10 minutes). Keep in the refrigerator until ready to use.

STRAWBERRY COMPOTE
100 g (3½ oz) strawberries
45 g (1½ oz) sugar
2 g (1/16 oz) pectin

STRAWBERRY – Place the strawberries, roughly chopped, with the sugar and pectin in a saucepan. Stir to combine. Cook over high heat, mashing the strawberries at the same time. Once the mixture is just below boiling point, lower the heat and simmer gently until it thickens (5–10 minutes). Keep in the refrigerator until ready to use.

CRÈME PÂTISSIÈRE

165 ml (5½ fl oz/⅔ cup)
full-cream milk
2 egg yolks
35 g (1¼ oz) sugar
8 g (³⁄₁₆ oz) plain (all-purpose)
flour
8 g (³⁄₁₆ oz) cornflour
½ pinch of salt
1 teaspoon calvados (optional)

CHANTILLY CREAM

250 ml (9 fl oz/1 cup) very cold
pouring (whipping) cream
25 g (1 oz) icing sugar
1 teaspoon natural vanilla
extract
1 teaspoon calvados (optional)

ICING

300 g (10½ oz) white fondant
icing, ready-made
yellow, blue and red food
colouring as desired

THE CRÈME PÂTISSIÈRE AND CHANTILLY CREAM

Make a plain crème pâtissière (see page 32) and a chantilly cream (see page 40). Keep in the refrigerator until ready to use. Add 125 g (4½ oz) of the chosen compote to the cooled crème pâtissière, whisking vigorously. Incorporate the chantilly cream.

ASSEMBLY

Pierce three holes in the base of the éclairs using a 6 mm nozzle. Fill a piping bag fitted with a plain 8 mm nozzle with the combined filling and start filling the éclairs from one of the ends. When the filling appears in the middle hole, finish filling from the other end.

THE ICING

On a very low heat, heat the fondant to lukewarm with a few drops of water, stirring. When the mixture is about 35°C (95°F), add a little lukewarm water until you have a mixture that falls back from the spatula without immediately merging with the rest of the fondant. Add food colouring to tint to the desired colour then remove from the heat. Dip the top of an éclair into the icing, then hold it vertically and run a finger over it to remove the excess icing. Run a finger around the edge of the icing so you have a nice clean edge. Ice the other éclairs in the same way.

Passionfruit, mandarin or strawberry éclairs (recipes page 84-86).

COCONUT ÉCLAIRS

4 sheets (8 g/³⁄₁₆ oz) gelatine
250 ml (9 fl oz/1 cup) pouring
(whipping) cream
60 g (2¼ oz) sugar
250 ml (9 fl oz/1 cup) coconut
milk

THE COCONUT CREAM

Soak the gelatine sheets in cold water. Scald the cream in a saucepan,
then remove from the heat. Squeeze out the excess liquid from the
gelatine, add it to the saucepan and whisk to dissolve it in the cream.
Add the sugar and whisk again. Pour in the coconut milk, stir, then
transfer to a bowl. Cover with plastic wrap placed in direct contact with
the cream and refrigerate until firm (allow 1–2 hours).

80 ml (2½ fl oz/⅓ cup) milk
80 ml (2½ fl oz/⅓ cup) water
70 g (2½ oz) butter
large pinch of salt
10 g (¼ oz) sugar
100 g (3½ oz/⅔ cup) plain
(all-purpose) flour
2 eggs

THE ÉCLAIRS

Preheat the oven to 150°C (300°F/Gas 2). Make the choux pastry (see
pages 24–27) and use it to fill a piping bag fitted with a plain 20 mm
nozzle. Position it at a 45 degree angle in relation to the baking tray and
push out the mixture while moving the bag in one clean movement to
give the éclair a nice straight shape; apply an even pressure to the piping
bag so that the tube of mixture that comes out of the nozzle has the same
diameter as the nozzle. When the éclair is 14 cm (5½ inches) long, cut off
the mixture with a smooth-bladed knife. If necessary, smooth the éclairs
with some of the beaten egg left over from making the pastry or else with
water. Bake for 55–60 minutes. Remove from the oven and allow to cool
on a wire rack.

ASSEMBLY

Pierce three holes in the base of the éclairs using a 6 mm nozzle or with
the tip of a ballpoint pen. Fill a piping bag fitted with a plain 8 mm nozzle
with the coconut cream and start filling the éclairs from one of the ends.
When the cream appears in the middle hole, finish filling from the other
end. Stop when the cream comes out the two other holes.

150 g (5½ oz) desiccated and/or
flaked coconut
300 g (10½ oz) white fondant
icing, ready-made

THE COCONUT ICING

Have the coconut ready on a plate. Over very low heat, heat the fondant
to lukewarm with a few drops of water, stirring constantly. When the
mixture is about 35°C/ 95°F (a little less than body temperature), add
a little lukewarm water until you have a mixture that falls back from the
spatula without immediately merging with the rest of the fondant. Remove
from the heat. Dip the top of an éclair in the icing, then hold it vertically
and run a finger over it to remove the excess icing. Run a finger around
the edge of the icing so you have a nice clean edge. Dip the éclair straight
away in the coconut. Ice and decorate the other éclairs in the same way.

VIOLET OR ROSE ÉCLAIRS

80 ml (2½ fl oz/⅓ cup) milk
80 ml (2½ fl oz/⅓ cup) water
70 g (2½ oz) butter
large pinch of salt
10 g (¼ oz) sugar
100 g (3½ oz/ ⅔ cup) plain
(all-purpose) flour
2 eggs
50 g (1¾ oz) pearl sugar
(optional)

VIOLET CRÈME PÂTISSIÈRE
410 ml (14¼ fl oz) full-cream
milk
5 egg yolks
80 g (2¾ oz) sugar
20 g (¾ oz) plain (all-purpose)
flour
20 g (¾ oz) cornflour
large pinch of salt
1 teaspoon violet essence

ROSE CHANTILLY CREAM
400 ml (14 fl oz) very cold
pouring (whipping) cream
40 g (1½ oz) icing sugar
1 teaspoon rosewater
red food colouring

ICING
300 g (10½ oz) white fondant
icing, ready-made
blue and red food colouring
10 crystallised rose petals
(optional)

THE ÉCLAIRS
Preheat the oven to 150°C (300°F/Gas 2). Make the choux pastry dough (see pages 24–27) and use it to fill a piping bag fitted with a plain 20 mm nozzle. Position it at a 45 degree angle in relation to the baking tray and push out the mixture while moving the bag in one clean movement to give the éclair a nice straight shape; apply an even pressure to the piping bag so that the tube of mixture that comes out of the nozzle has the same diameter as the nozzle. When the éclair is 14 cm (5½ inches) long, cut off the mixture with a smooth-bladed knife. If necessary, smooth the éclairs with some of the beaten egg left over from making the pastry or else with water. For the rose éclairs, scatter over the pearl sugar, if using, then tip up the tray to remove the excess sugar. Bake for 55–60 minutes. Remove from the oven and allow to cool on a wire rack.

THE FILLING
Choose one of the following filling and decorating methods for each batch of 6 to 8 éclairs.
VIOLET – Make a plain crème pâtissière (see page 32). Once it has cooled, add violet essence and whisk vigorously until the mixture is soft and creamy.
ROSE – Make a chantilly cream (see page 40). Add, before starting to whisk, the rosewater and red food colouring to make a pale pink colour.

ASSEMBLY AND DECORATION
VIOLET – When the éclairs are cool, use a piping bag fitted with a plain 8 mm nozzle to fill them with violet crème pâtissière (see page 30). Over very low heat, heat the fondant to lukewarm with a few drops of water, stirring. When the mixture is about 35°C/95°F, add a little lukewarm water until you have a mixture that falls from the spatula without immediately merging with the rest of the fondant. Tint with food colouring to the desired colour, then remove from the heat. Dip the top of an éclair into the icing, hold it vertically and run a finger over it to remove the excess icing. Run a finger around the edge of the icing so you have a nice clean edge.
ROSE – When the éclairs are cool, slice them in half lengthways using a serrated knife. Whisk the chantilly cream one last time so that it is quite firm and use it to fill a piping bag fitted with a 16 mm star nozzle. Fill the éclairs generously, then place the lids back on top and press lightly. Scatter with some crystallised rose petals, if desired.

TONKA BEAN OR SALTED-BUTTER CARAMEL ÉCLAIRS

Salted-butter caramel needs no introduction; here it is both inside the éclair and on top of it.
Tonka bean, for its part, gives a subtle bitter-almond flavour to this very refined chocolate éclair.

CHOCOLATE-TONKA CRÈME PÂTISSIÈRE

55 g (2 oz) pouring (whipping) cream
65 g (2¼ oz) dark chocolate
165 g (5¼ oz/²⁄₃ cup) full-cream milk
tonka bean
35 g (1¼ oz) sugar
2 egg yolks
½ pinch of salt
8 g (³⁄₁₆ oz) plain (all-purpose) flour
8 g (³⁄₁₆ oz) cornflour

SALTED-BUTTER CARAMEL CRÈME PÂTISSIÈRE

20 g (¾ oz) water
60 g (2¼ oz) sugar
55 g (2 oz) pouring (whipping) cream
10 g (¼ oz) salted butter
165 g (5¼ oz) full-cream milk
20 g (¾ oz) sugar
2 egg yolks
½ pinch of salt
8 g (³⁄₁₆ oz) plain (all-purpose) flour
8 g (³⁄₁₆ oz) cornflour

THE CRÈME PÂTISSIÈRE

Choose one of the following filling and icing methods for each batch of 6 to 8 éclairs.

CHOCOLATE–TONKA – Scald the cream (heat until just below boiling point) in a saucepan and pour it over the chocolate, broken into pieces in a heat resistant bowl. Stir until you have a thick ganache. Set aside. Bring the milk to the boil with the tonka bean. Remove from the heat, cover and allow to infuse for 5–10 minutes. Make a crème pâtissière (see page 32) using this infused milk and the remaining ingredients, removing the bean before incorporating the egg yolks. Combine the warm crème pâtissière with the ganache, cover with plastic film placed in direct contact with the crème to prevent it forming a skin and refrigerate.

SALTED-BUTTER CARAMEL – Pour the water and sugar into a heavy-based saucepan. Wait until the sugar has absorbed the water (a few seconds), cover and bring to the boil over high heat, monitoring the colour from time to time. Heat the cream in a separate saucepan. When the caramel is dark enough, remove it from the heat and add the hot cream all at once. Whisk until smooth, incorporate the salted butter, diced, off the heat and set aside. Make a crème pâtissière (see page 32). Incorporate the caramel into the crème when it is still warm, cover with plastic film placed in direct contact with the crème to prevent it forming a skin and refrigerate.

continued >

> continued from previous page

80 ml (2½ fl oz/⅓ cup) milk
80 ml (2½ fl oz/⅓ cup) water
70 g (2½ oz) butter
large pinch of salt
10 g (¼ oz) sugar
100 g (3½ oz/⅔ cup) flour
2 eggs

THE ÉCLAIRS

Preheat the oven to 150°C (300°F/Gas 2). Make the choux pastry dough and pipe the éclairs onto a baking tray (see pages 24–29). Place in the oven and cook for 55–60 minutes. Remove from the oven and allow to cool on a wire rack.

Fill a piping bag fitted with a plain 8 mm nozzle, with chocolate–tonka or salted-butter caramel crème pâtissière as desired, then fill the éclairs (see page 30).

125 g (4½ oz) dark chocolate
50 g (1¾ oz) butter
40 g (1½ oz) honey
125 g (4½ oz) pouring
(whipping) cream
extra dark chocolate, melted,
to decorate

THE ICING

CHOCOLATE GANACHE – Break the chocolate into pieces into a heatproof bowl that's large enough to hold an éclair. Add the butter, diced, and the honey. Scald the cream (heat until just below boiling point) in a saucepan. Remove from heat and pour into the bowl over the chocolate. Combine with a flexible spatula. If the mixture isn't completely melted, pour 1 cm (½ inch) water into the saucepan used for the cream and bring to the boil, then remove from the heat. Place the bowl on top and stir until the ganache is smooth. Dip the top of the éclairs into the ganache. Set aside in the refrigerator. Once the icing has set, stripe the éclairs with melted chocolate as indicated in the photo.

90 g (3¼ oz) sugar
30 g (1 oz) water
50 g (1¾ oz) pouring
(whipping) cream
15 g (½ oz) salted butter

SALTED-BUTTER CARAMEL – Make a caramel as described for the crème pâtissière on page 92. Once the butter has been incorporated, allow the caramel to cool to lukewarm. Take some caramel with a spoon, place it on an éclair and spread it out using your finger.

MILLE FEUILLE-STYLE ÉCLAIRS

80 ml (2½ fl oz/⅓ cup) milk
80 ml (2½ fl oz/⅓ cup) water
70 g (2½ oz) butter
large pinch of salt
10 g (¼ oz) sugar
100 g (3½ oz/⅔ cup) plain (all-purpose) flour
2 eggs

THE ÉCLAIRS

Preheat the oven to 150°C (300°F/Gas 2). Make the choux pastry dough (see pages 24–27) and use it to fill a piping bag fitted with a plain 20 mm nozzle. Position the nozzle at a 45 degree angle in relation to the baking tray and push out the mixture while moving the bag in one clean movement to give the éclair a nice straight shape; apply an even pressure to the piping bag so that the tube of mixture that comes out of the nozzle has the same diameter as the nozzle. When the éclair is 14 cm (5½ inches) long, cut off the mixture with a smooth-bladed knife. If necessary, smooth the éclairs with some of the beaten egg left over from making the pastry or else with water. Bake for 55–60 minutes. Remove from the oven and allow to cool on a wire rack.

CRÈME PÂTISSIÈRE

½ vanilla bean
170 ml (5½ fl oz/⅔ cup) full-cream milk
2 egg yolks
35 g (1¼ oz) sugar
8 g (³⁄₁₆ oz) plain (all-purpose) flour
8 g (³⁄₁₆ oz) cornflour
½ pinch of salt
1 teaspoon rum, Grand Marnier or calvados (optional)

THE LIGHT VANILLA CREAM FILLING

Split the vanilla bean and scrape out the seeds. Add them, as well as the bean, to the milk with half the sugar in a saucepan. Bring to the boil and, as soon as boiling point is reached, remove from the heat, cover and allow to infuse for 5–10 minutes. Make the crème pâtissière (see page 32) with this infused milk and the remaining ingredients except the alcohol (remove vanilla bean from the milk before mixing with the eggs). Once the crème has completely cooled, add the alcohol as desired, whisking vigorously, then keep in the refrigerator, covered with plastic wrap until ready to use. Make a chantilly cream (see page 40). Whisk the crème pâtissière and the chantilly cream together to combine. Cover and refrigerate.

CHANTILLY CREAM

250 ml (9 fl oz/1 cup) very cold pouring (whipping) cream
25 g (1 oz) icing sugar
1 teaspoon natural vanilla extract

ASSEMBLY

Pierce three holes in the base of the éclairs using a 6 mm nozzle or with the tip of a ballpoint pen. Fill a piping bag fitted with a plain 8 mm nozzle with the light vanilla cream and fill the éclairs from one of the ends. When the cream appears in the middle hole, finish filling from the other end. Stop when the cream comes out the two other holes.

60 g (2¼ oz) chocolate
300 g (10½ oz) white fondant
icing, ready-made

MILLE FEUILLE ICING

Melt the chocolate in a saucepan over low heat and keep it warm over very low heat so it stays liquid. Over very low heat, heat the fondant to lukewarm with a few drops of water, stirring constantly. When the mixture is about 35°C/95°F (a little lower than body temperature), add a little lukewarm water until you have an icing that drops from the spatula without immediately merging with the rest of the fondant. Remove from the heat. Dip the top of an éclair into the icing, then hold it vertically and run a finger over it to remove the excess icing. Run a finger around the edge of the icing so you have a nice clean edge. Without waiting too long, drop a thin line of melted chocolate on the éclair by running it off a spoon, and draw several parallel diagonal lines (careful! the spoon mustn't touch the fondant). If desired, use a toothpick or the point of a knife to drag the chocolate to either side of each line, making small perpendicular marks. Ice the remaining éclairs in the same way making sure you stir the fondant well before each dipping.

CHOCOLATE SHELL ICE-CREAM ÉCLAIRS

80 ml (2½ fl oz/⅓ cup) milk
80 ml (2½ fl oz/⅓ cup) water
70 g (2½ oz) butter
large pinch of salt
10 g (¼ oz) sugar
100 g (3½ oz/⅔ cup) plain
(all-purpose) flour
2 eggs

THE ÉCLAIRS

Preheat the oven to 150°C (300°F/Gas 2). Make the choux pastry dough (see pages 24–27) and use it to fill a piping bag fitted with a plain 20 mm nozzle. Position the nozzle at a 45 degree angle in relation to the baking tray and push out the mixture while moving the bag in one clean movement to give the éclair a nice straight shape; apply an even pressure to the piping bag so that the tube of mixture that comes out of the nozzle has the same diameter as the nozzle. When the éclair is 14 cm (5½ inches) long, cut off the mixture with a smooth-bladed knife. If necessary, smooth the éclairs with some of the beaten egg left over from making the pastry or else with water. Bake for 55–60 minutes. Remove from the oven and allow to cool on a wire rack.

500 ml (17 fl oz/2 cups) vanilla
ice cream

THE FILLING

Take the ice cream out of the freezer. When the éclairs are cool, slice them in half lengthways with a serrated knife. Work the ice cream with a spatula to soften it, then use a spoon to fill the éclairs with ice cream, mounding the ice cream a little. Replace the lid of the éclairs, pressing down very lightly and place in the freezer for 15 minutes (they need to be very cold but not frozen).

250 g (9 oz) white, milk or dark
chocolate
2 teaspoons neutral-flavoured
oil (peanut, grapeseed or
sunflower)

THE CHOCOLATE SHELL

Melt the chocolate in a saucepan over low heat with the oil and mix to make smooth. Take the éclairs out of the freezer and place them on a wire rack set over baking paper or a baking tray to catch the excess. Pour the hot chocolate over the cold éclairs in a rapid motion so that you cover them completely. So that the layer of chocolate is thin, avoid going over the same spot several times. Wait a few moments so that the chocolate sets and serve immediately or keep them in the freezer.

SALAMMBÔ
THE LITTLE UPSIDE-DOWN ÉCLAIR

For lovers of custard profiteroles with caramel, this decadent little éclair
is named for a famous nineteenth-century novel by Gustave Flaubert.

250 g (9 oz) full-cream milk
50 g (1¾ oz) sugar
½ vanilla bean
3 egg yolks
pinch of salt
10 g (¼ oz) plain (all-purpose)
flour
10 g (¼ oz) cornflour
(cornstarch)

THE CRÈME PÂTISSIÈRE
Pour the milk into a saucepan with half the sugar. Split the vanilla bean and
scrape out the seeds with the back of a knife blade. Add the seeds, as well
as the bean, to the milk. Whisk the egg yolks with the remaining sugar and
the salt, add the flour and the cornflour, and mix well. Heat the milk. Just
before it reaches boiling point, remove from the heat, pour a little milk into
the egg mixture and whisk vigorously. Transfer the mixture to the saucepan
and whisk until smooth. Place back onto the heat and bring to the boil
while continuing to whisk, then let it boil until it firstly thickens, and then
reaches a second stage of being thick but fluid. Stop the cooking process
at this stage. Pour onto a plate, remove the vanilla bean and cover with
plastic wrap placed in direct contact with the crème to avoid a skin forming.

40 ml (1¼ fl oz) milk
40 ml (1¼ fl oz) water
35 g (1¼ oz) butter
pinch salt
5 g (⅛ oz) sugar
50 g (1¾ oz/⅓ cup) plain
(all-purpose) flour
1 egg

THE ÉCLAIRS
Preheat the oven to 150°C (300°F/Gas 2). Make the choux pastry dough
(see pages 24–27) and use it to fill a piping bag fitted with a plain 12 mm
nozzle. Position the bag at a 45 degree angle in relation to the baking tray
and squeeze, keeping the nozzle against the mixture, until a slightly wide
choux bun shape forms. Then move the nozzle backwards and continue
this shape for the length of about half an éclair, or 7 cm (2¾ inches). Bake
in the oven for 50–55 minutes, then remove the tray from the oven and
remove the éclairs from the tray to cool.

continued >

> continued from previous page

60 g (2¼ oz) flaked almonds

THE ALMONDS

Increase the temperature of the oven to 160°C (315°F/Gas 2–3). Spread almonds on a baking tray and place them in the oven for about 10 minutes, until they are nice and golden.

1 tablespoon Grand Marnier

ASSEMBLY

Add the Grand Marnier to the cooled crème pâtissière and whisk vigorously until the mixture is soft and creamy. Taste and add more Grand Marnier if necessary. Pierce the top of the éclairs using a 6 mm nozzle or the tip of a ballpoint pen. Fill them with the crème pâtissière using a piping bag fitted with a plain nozzle, 8 mm in diameter (see page 30); fill them as much as possible and wipe off the excess crème on the side of a bowl.

150 g (5½ oz) sugar
50 g (1¼ oz) water
neutral-flavoured oil (peanut, grapeseed, sunflower)

THE ICING

Make the caramel according to the instructions given on page 50. Coat a tray with a very thin layer of oil spread using a sheet of paper towel and arrange the flaked almonds, three by three, in star shapes. Dip the underside (the smooth base) of a salammbô in the caramel then, without draining off the excess caramel, place the salammbô immediately on an almond star. Proceed in the same way for each of the others, then detach them from the tray and serve them turned back over, with the almonds on the top.

CARAMEL ICE-CREAM ÉCLAIRS

80 ml (2½ fl oz/⅓ cup) milk
80 ml (2½ fl oz/⅓ cup) water
70 g (2½ oz) butter
large pinch of salt
10 g (¼ oz) sugar
100 g (3½ oz/⅔ cup) plain
(all-purpose) flour
2 eggs

THE ÉCLAIRS

Preheat the oven to 150°C (300°F/Gas 2). Make the choux pastry dough (see pages 24–27) and use it to fill a piping bag fitted with a plain 20 mm nozzle. Position it at a 45 degree angle in relation to the baking tray and push out the mixture while moving the bag in one clean movement to give the éclair a nice straight shape; apply an even pressure to the piping bag so that the tube of mixture that comes out of the nozzle has the same diameter as the nozzle. When the éclair is 14 cm (5½ inches) long, cut off the mixture with a smooth-bladed knife. If necessary, smooth the éclairs with some of the beaten egg left over from making the pastry or else with water. Bake for 55–60 minutes. Remove from the oven and allow to cool on a wire rack.

500 ml (17 fl oz/2 cups)
caramel ice cream

THE FILLING

Take the ice cream out of the freezer. When the éclairs are cool, slice them in half lengthways with a serrated knife. Work the ice cream with a spatula to soften it. Fill the éclairs using a teaspoon or a piping bag with a plain 12 mm nozzle, mounding the ice cream a little. Replace the lid of the éclairs, pressing down on them very gently and place in the freezer for just the time it takes to prepare the caramel.

90 ml (3 fl oz) pouring
(whipping) cream
30 ml (1 fl oz) water
90 g (3¼ oz) sugar
15 g (½ oz) salted butter

THE ICING

Scald the cream (heat to just below boiling point) in a saucepan and set aside. Place the water, then the sugar, in a small heavy-based saucepan. Wait until the sugar has absorbed the water (a few seconds), cover and then bring to the boil. Allow the caramel to colour, checking from time to time. Once the caramel has reached a lovely mahogany colour (reddish-brown) take the saucepan off the heat, add the hot cream all at once and stir with a spatula. If the mixture isn't perfectly smooth, place the saucepan back over medium heat for 2 minutes, stirring constantly. Add the salted butter in small pieces off the heat. Mix well. Take the éclairs out of the freezer and place them on a wire rack set over baking paper or a baking tray to catch the excess. Drizzle them with caramel and serve immediately or keep them in the freezer.

Chocolate shell ice-cream éclair (see page 98), left, and caramel ice-cream éclair.

MINI ÉCLAIRS

Prepare the selected fillings as per the instructions given on pages as referenced. Preheat oven to 150°C (300°F/Gas 2). Make the choux pastry dough (see pages 24–27), use it to fill a piping bag fitted with a plain 16 mm nozzle and pipe éclairs, 5–6 cm (2–2½ inches) in length, onto a baking tray. Bake for 45–50 minutes. Allow to cool, then fill mini éclairs and apply the icings.

LIME (page 78)
LIME CRÈME PÂTISSIÈRE
85 ml (2 ¼ fl oz) full-cream milk
1 egg yolk
15 g (½ oz) sugar
5 g (⅛ oz) plain (all-purpose)
   flour
5 g (⅛ oz) cornflour
small pinch of salt
1 lime
LIME ICING
100 g (3½ oz) white fondant icing
yellow and blue food colouring

COCONUT (page 88)
COCONUT CREAM
60 ml (2 fl oz/¼ cup) coconut
   milk
60 ml (2 fl oz/¼ cup) pouring
   (whipping) cream
15 g (½ oz) sugar
1 gelatine sheet
COCONUT ICING
100 g (3½ oz) white fondant icing
40 g (1½ oz) desiccated or flaked
   coconut

PASSIONFRUIT (page 84)
CRÈME PÂTISSIÈRE
85 ml (2¼ fl oz) full-cream milk
1 egg yolk
15 g (½ oz) sugar
5 g (⅛ oz) plain (all-purpose)
   flour
5 g (⅛ oz) cornflour
small pinch of salt
CHANTILLY CREAM
125 ml (4 fl oz/½ cup) pouring
   (whipping) cream
10 g (¼ oz) icing sugar
1 teaspoon natural vanilla extract
PASSIONFRUIT COMPOTE
5 passionfruit
35 g (1¼ oz) sugar
1 g (pinch) pectin
FONDANT ICING
100 g (3½ oz) white fondant
   icing, ready-made
yellow food colouring

STRAWBERRY (page 84)
CRÈME PÂTISSIÈRE
85 ml (2¼ fl oz) full-cream milk
1 egg yolk
15 g (½ oz) sugar
5 g (⅛ oz) plain (all-purpose)
   flour
5 g (⅛ oz) cornflour
small pinch of salt
CHANTILLY CREAM
125 ml (4 fl oz/½ cup) pouring
   (whipping) cream
10 g (¼ oz) icing sugar
1 teaspoon natural vanilla extract
STRAWBERRY COMPOTE
50 g (1¼ oz) strawberries
20 g (¾ oz) sugar
1 g (pinch) pectin
FONDANT ICING
100 g (3½ oz) white fondant icing
pink food colouring

continued >

Food colouring can tint the icing an appropriate colour to match
the filling... or any colour you like!

Use traditional chocolate ganache, coffee fondant or caramel icing, or use your imagination!

> continued from previous page

CHOC-ORANGE (page 80)

ORANGE CRÈME PÂTISSIÈRE
85 ml (2¼ fl oz) full-cream milk
1 egg yolk
15 g (½ oz) sugar
5 g (⅛ oz) plain (all-purpose)
    flour
5 g (⅛ oz) cornflour
pinch of salt
1 orange
CHOCOLATE SHELL
125 g (4½ oz) dark chocolate
1 teaspoon neutral-flavoured oil

CHOCOLATE (page 60-63)

CHOCOLATE CRÈME
    PÂTISSIÈRE
85 ml (2¼ fl oz) full-cream milk
1 egg yolk
15 g (½ oz) sugar
5 g (⅛ oz) plain (all-purpose)
    flour
5 g (⅛ oz) cornflour
small pinch of salt
60 g (2¼ oz) chocolate ganache
CHOCOLATE GANACHE
    (filling and icing)
65 g (2⅜ oz) pouring (whipping)
    cream
65 g (2⅜ oz) chocolate
20 g (¾ oz) honey
25 g (1 oz) butter
1 teaspoon Grand Marnier

COFFEE (pages 60-63)

COFFEE CRÈME PÂTISSIÈRE
85 ml (2¼ fl oz) full-cream milk
1 egg yolk
15 g (½ oz) sugar
5 g (⅛ oz) plain (all-purpose)
    flour
5 g (⅛ oz) cornflour
pinch of salt
1 teaspoon coffee essence
COFFEE ICING
100 g (3½ oz) white fondant
    icing, ready-made
1-2 teaspoons coffee essence
yellow food colouring (optional)

CARAMEL (pages 92-95)

CARAMEL CRÈME
    PÂTISSIÈRE
85 ml (2¼ fl oz) full-cream milk
1 egg yolk
15 g (½ oz) sugar
5 g (⅛ oz) plain (all-purpose)
    flour
5 g (⅛ oz) cornflour
small pinch of salt
15 g (½ oz) water
30 g (1 oz) sugar
30 g (1 oz) pouring (whipping)
    cream
5 g (⅛ oz) salted butter
SALTED-BUTTER CARAMEL
60 g (2¼ oz) sugar
20 ml (½ fl oz) water
35 g (1¼ oz) pouring (whipping)
    cream
10 g (¼ oz) salted butter

GLOSSARY

BINDING
The action of thickening a preparation or sauce by adding, for example, flour, egg yolks, cream.

BOILING (AND SCALDING)
A mixture is boiling when it is over high heat and large bubbles appear on the surface. The mixture is at a higher temperature than one that is scalded (just below boiling point), whose surface seems to tremble.

COLLAPSING
Mixture or pastry that falls after rising. For example: choux pastry collapses, egg whites collapse.

DOUBLE BOILING
Mode of cooking or reheating over a container partly filled with boiling water. For example: to melt chocolate, pour 1 cm (½ inch) water into a saucepan and bring to the boil, then remove from the heat and place a heat-resistant bowl containing the chocolate over the saucepan; the bowl mustn't touch the water or the base of the saucepan, but it should go in a fair way.

DUSTING
Cover by scattering over a powder-like substance (icing (confectioners') sugar, cocoa powder).

FLAVOURING
To add a flavour in liquid form (natural vanilla extract, for example) or solid form (cocoa, for example) to a mixture in order to give it a particular taste.

GELATINE
Translucent substance derived from the denaturation of collagen protein. It is sold in sheet and powder form, and is used in many preparations for its gelling effect.

GLUTEN
Elastic network formed by insoluble proteins contained in flour under the effect of kneading and contact with water. Gluten gives elasticity to a dough.

INCORPORATE
Add one ingredient to another and mix to combine.

INFUSING
The immersion of an ingredient (vanilla bean, tea leaves, citrus zest, tonka bean) into a hot liquid close to the boil, followed by gradual cooling, the aim being to flavour the liquid.

PANADE
Name given to the choux pastry mixture before the eggs are incorporated.

RELAXING
Said of a pastry or cream that softens after being kneaded, moistened or after a certain degree of cooking.

SIFTING
The action of passing a substance through a sieve to remove lumps. For example: flour, icing sugar.

STARCH
A complex carbohydrate found in many plants since it forms their store of energy. The starch in flour is what makes pastry dough viscous.

VISCOSITY
Resistance of a fluid to flowing freely. The thicker a liquid is, the less easily it flows, and the more it is said to be viscous.

WHISKING
To use a whisk to mix a preparation, bind it, lighten it or make it frothy (meringue, whipped cream).

WORKING
To beat or stir a preparation by hand, whisk, spatula or machine.

ZESTING
To remove the thin coloured membrane of a lemon, lime or orange to extract its flavour, using a special knife, or a zester, or by another method.

SECRETS OF ECLAIRS

INDEX

ACKNOWLEDGEMENTS

Thanks to Emmanuel Levallois and Rose-Marie Di Domenico. The recipes are mine, but the book is yours!
Thanks to Pauline Labrousse, my new editor, for her investment in this project. Her recipe ideas, her
investigations of various Parisian pâtisseries, her very careful reading of my writing ... I felt like I had
a colleague, which is a change from the "solitude of the author"!
Thanks to Olivier Malingue for his talent as a photographer and as a decorator of choux pastries!
Thanks to my mother, Stéphanie, for looking after my son Antoine on so many occasions: I knew
he was in good hands and I could work with my mind at ease!
Thanks to Apollonia Poilâne and Alain Selmersheim for their friendship and advice concerning
each of my books.

BIBLIOGRAPHY

Le Livre du Pâtissier, Bernard Deschamps and Jean-Claude Deschaintre,
    Éditions Jacques Lanore, 2004
Analyse des phénomènes and transformations culinaires, Bruno Cardinale
    and René van Sevenant, Éditions LT Jacques Lanore, 2010
On Food and Cooking, Harold McGee, Scribner, 2004
BakeWise, Shirley O. Corriher, Scribner, 2008